The
Oxford Book of
Irish Verse

The
Oxford Book of
Irish Verse

XVIIth Century–XXth Century

Chosen by

Donagh MacDonagh

and

Lennox Robinson

Oxford

At the Clarendon Press

Oxford University Press, Amen House, London E.C.4

GLASGOW NEW YORK TORONTO MELBOURNE WELLINGTON
BOMBAY CALCUTTA MADRAS KARACHI KUALA LUMPUR
CAPE TOWN IBADAN NAIROBI ACCRA

FIRST EDITION 1958
REPRINTED (WITH CORRECTIONS) 1959

PRINTED IN GREAT BRITAIN

PREFACE

In 1900 Stopford A. Brooke and T. W. Rolleston, both poets in their own right, published *A Treasury of Irish Poetry*. They dedicated the book to Sir Charles Gavan Duffy for 'the publishing of the first worthy collection of Irish national poetry'. The book occupied nearly 600 pages and as well as an introduction contained short biographical material. Yeats wrote of Lionel Johnson, Althea Giles and of Æ; Æ of William Larminie; T. W. Rolleston of Yeats; Macneile Dixon of Edward Dowden; and Rolleston of Francis Savage Armstrong. Since then there have been other anthologies, notably *The Dublin Book of Irish Verse*, edited by John Cook and published in 1909 by Hodges-Figgis, and *A Golden Treasury of Irish Verse*, edited by myself and published by Macmillan in 1925. There has been a notable and comprehensive anthology made by Kathleen Hoagland and published by the Devin-Adair Company in the U.S.A., and of works on a smaller scale Geoffrey Taylor's *Irish Poets of the Nineteenth Century* should be noted.

But much fine poetry has been written in Ireland during the past twenty or thirty years; moreover tastes change, so the time seemed ripe for a new anthology going back to the earliest times and finishing the day before yesterday. The editors may have seemed a little unkind to some of the well-established old poets, leaving out some loved Moore or some favourite Mangan. But Moore and Ferguson are easily to be found in all our public libraries and if we seem inadequately to represent them it is to make room for the others, the ones who died only yesterday or the ones whose best work lies in the future.

When over thirty years ago I compiled *The Golden*

PREFACE

Treasury of Irish Verse I had as helpers and critics Æ and
W. B. Yeats. This volume is the work of a young poet
and an old lover of Irish verse.

LENNOX ROBINSON

ACKNOWLEDGEMENTS

THE editors wish to thank all those who have kindly given their permission to include copyright material. They are:

Mrs. E. Humphreys and Mr. Donn S. Piatt for the poem by George Sigerson; Mrs. Honor Stopford Drysdale for the poem by T. W. Rolleston; Mrs. D. Long for the poem by Dora Sigerson Shorter; Miss Pamela Hinkson for four poems by Katherine Tynan; the Executor and Trustee for five poems by Douglas Hyde; Mrs. W. B. Yeats; Mr. P. J. Little for the poem by Philip Little; Mr. Diarmuid Russell for four poems by Æ (George W. Russell); Mr. Seumas O'Sullivan; Mr. Simon Campbell for four poems by Joseph Campbell; Mr. Seumas MacManus for the poem by Alice Milligan; Mrs. Blanaid Salkeld; Mrs. I. M. Flower; the Executors of the James Joyce Estate; Dr. Padraic Colum; Mrs. James Stephens; Mr. Arthur L. Rye and Mr. Clifford Bax for the poem by Sir Arnold Bax ('Dermot O'Byrne'); Monsignor Patrick Browne; Mr. Brinsley MacNamara; Mrs. Geoffrey Taylor; Mr. Thomas McGreevy; Mr. Robert Graves; Mr. Austin Clarke; the author's executors for five poems by F. R. Higgins; Mr. Francis MacManus; Dr. Monk Gibbon; the Reverend A. L. Wilson; Dr. Patrick MacDonogh; The Earl of Longford; Mr. George Buchanan for three poems by John Lyle Donaghy; Miss Rhoda Coghill; Mr. Frank O'Connor; Mr. Ewart Milne; Mr. Patrick Kavanagh; Mr. Cecil Day-Lewis; Mr. Bryan Guinness; Miss Sheila Wingfield; Mr. Padraic Fallon; His Excellency Denis Devlin; Mr. Robert Farren; Mr. Brian O Nolan; Mr. Leslie Daiken; Mr. Niall Sheridan; Miss Máire MacEntee; Mr. Roy MacFadden; Mr. Thomas Kinsella; the Society of Authors for four poems by Katherine Tynan and one poem by Thomas McGreevy; Messrs. Curtis Brown Ltd. for two poems by Lord Dunsany.

We are also indebted to the following publishers: Messrs. Routledge & Kegan Paul for permission to include two poems by Edward Dowden; the Talbot Press for one poem by Percy French, three poems by Joseph Plunkett, and one poem by Padraic Pearse; Messrs. Constable & Co. Ltd. for permission to quote five poems from *Collected Poems* by Oliver St. John Gogarty, three poems from *Ancient Irish Poetry* by Kuno Meyer, and one poem from *Mediaeval Latin Lyrics* by Helen Waddell; Messrs. Chatto & Windus Ltd. for

ACKNOWLEDGEMENTS

the poem by Eleanor Hull from *Poem Book of the Gael*; Messrs. Jonathan Cape Ltd. for 'Jean Richepin's Song' from *Selected Poems* by Herbert Trench, for 'I Hear an Army' and 'What Counsel has the Hooded Moon' from *Chamber Music* by James Joyce, and for 'The Poet' and 'Jig' from *Poems in Wartime* and 'The Album' from *Word Over All* by C. Day-Lewis; Messrs. George Allen & Unwin Ltd. for four poems from J. M. Synge's *Poems and Translation* and for two pages from J. M. Synge's *The Playboy of the Western World*; Messrs. G. Gill & Son for the poem by Alice Milligan from *We Sang for Ireland, Poems of Ethna Carbery, Alice Milligan and Seumas MacManus*; Messrs. Herbert Jenkins Ltd. for five poems from *The Complete Poems of Francis Ledwidge*; Messrs. Cassell & Co. for six poems by Robert Graves from *Collected Poems* (1914–47); the Orwell Press for three poems by Patrick MacDonogh; Messrs. John Lane The Bodley Head Ltd. for 'Evergreen' by Ewart Milne from *Diamond Cut Diamond* and for the passage from *Ulysses* by James Joyce; the Hogarth Press for three poems from *Collected Poems* (1954) by C. Day-Lewis; Kalakshetra Publications for two poems by J. H. Cousins; the Cresset Press for the poem by Sheila Wingfield; Messrs. Faber & Faber Ltd. for six poems from the *Collected Poems* of Louis MacNeice, three poems from *The Hungry Grass* by Donagh MacDonagh, the passages from *Finnegans Wake*, and 'Tutto e Sciolto' by James Joyce from *Pomes Pennyeach*; Messrs. Martin Secker & Warburg Ltd. for five poems by W. R. Rodgers; Messrs. Sheed & Ward Ltd. for five poems by Robert Farren from *Rime, Gentlemen, Please* and *The First Exile*; the Dolmen Press for four poems by Thomas Kinsella; Messrs. Macmillan & Co. Ltd. for four poems by James Stephens from his *Collected Poems*, five poems by F. R. Higgins from *The Gap of Brightness* and *The Dark Breed*, four poems by George W. Russell (Æ) from *Selected Poems*, and two poems from *The Fountain of Magic* by Frank O'Connor. The poems by W. B. Yeats are taken from his *Collected Poems* published by Macmillan.

We would like to express our thanks to the following American publishers for permission to include material copyright in the United States: the Macmillan Company, New York, for four poems from the *Collected Poems* of James Stephens and for the poems by W. B. Yeats: they are taken from *Poetical Works*, Volume I ('The Stolen Child', 'Down by the Salley Gardens', 'To Ireland in the Coming Times'), *In the Seven Woods* ('Red Hanrahan's Song about Ireland'), *Later Poems from Michael Robartes and Dancer* ('Easter, 1916',

ACKNOWLEDGEMENTS

'The Second Coming'), *In the Winding Stair* ('In Memory of Eva Gore-Booth and Con Markiewicz' and 'Coole Park'), *The Tower* ('Sailing to Byzantium'), *Last Poems and Plays* ('Under Ben Bulben'); the Devin-Adair Company for four poems by Padraic Colum from *The Collected Poems of Padraic Colum*, copyright 1916, 1922, 1927, 1930, 1932, 1953 by Padraic Colum, and for poems by J. L. Donaghy Monk Gibbon, for five poems from *The Collected Poems of Oliver St. John Gogarty*, 1954, Patrick Kavanagh, Patrick MacDonogh, Mary Davenport O'Neill, Blanaid Salkeld, Eileen Shanahan, and Dora Sigerson Shorter, which previously appeared in *1000 Years of Irish Poetry* and *New Irish Poets*; Random House Inc. for the excerpts from *Ulysses* by James Joyce (copyright 1914, 1918, 1942, 1946 by Norah Joyce) and from *The Playboy of the Western World* from *The Complete Works of John M. Synge* (copyright 1935 by the Modern Library), together with the four poems by J. M. Synge (copyright 1909 and renewed 1936 by the executors of the author) and six poems by Louis MacNeice (copyright 1937, 1938, 1940 by Louis MacNeice) from *Poems 1925–1940*; the Viking Press Inc. for permission to include the excerpts from *Finnegans Wake* and the three poems by James Joyce; Sheed & Ward Inc. for Robert Farren's poems 'The Pets' and 'The Mason' from *This Man was Ireland* (copyright 1943), 'The Beset Wife' from *Time's Wall Asunder*, and 'No Woman Born' and 'All That is and Can Delight' from *Rime, Gentlemen, Please* (copyright 1945); Doubleday & Co. Inc. for six poems from *Collected Poems* by Robert Graves; the Oxford University Press Inc., New York, for four poems from *Short is the Time* by C. Day-Lewis; Farrar, Straus & Cudahy Inc. for four poems by W. R. Rodgers from *Europa and the Bull*; Harcourt, Brace & Company Inc. for 'Life's Circumnavigators' by W. R. Rodgers.

Grateful thanks are also due to Mr. Brendan Glynn, of Pearse Street Library, Dublin, who helped in tracing rare books, and to Mr. Patrick Funge, who helped with the proofs.

INTRODUCTION

I

DURING the centuries when Ireland was a nation on the run only the portable arts could survive. Sculpture, symphonic music, the plastic arts all need fosterage, peace, security, and wealth to grow and survive: but a poem, a story, or a song may be carried safely inside a mind, can be handed on, preserved, and ornamented. Having no printing works or binderies our literature was the nursling of memory—and it was in Irish. In English little of value was written before the turn of the nineteenth century, and such verse as was written was for an English audience.

To understand why Irish poetry in English is a relatively novel art it is only necessary to know that English as the vernacular language of the country is little more than three centuries old, that the imaginative thought of the people and their poets was in Irish and that the only English known by the majority was that minimum necessary to understand an order.

The attempt to subjugate Ireland which began in the twelfth century had two main objects: to make the island a pacific colony accepting English rule and law, and to suppress the native law and language which were inimical to the new order. The first object never completely succeeded, the second succeeded only incompletely until after the Battle of the Boyne in 1690, except in small pockets around the garrison towns, and in the Pale. There were therefore two and sometimes three languages existing side by side, occasionally overlapping, but mutually exclusive —Norman-French, Anglo-Saxon, and Irish—and there was little intercourse of thought or culture between the two races. There was loss on both sides. The native Irish, knowing no English, missed the great period of transition when English was evolving as a language, missed the ballad as a seminal source of poetry, and missed the opportunity, which might have been to the advantage of English, of adding new words to the new language—there are notably few Irish loan-words in English, despite the proximity of the islands and the enforced intercourse. The English invaders lost a world of myth and romance and the Irish verse-forms which might have further enriched the English language.

Few of the Irish poets before Ferguson knew any Irish, though Swift was sufficiently interested to have Hugh MacGowran translate for him into English prose his rollicking song of feasting, MacGowran having given the Dean his choice of English or Latin. Swift re-Englished the song:

> O'Rourke's noble fare
> Will ne'er be forgot
> By those who were there
> And those who were not.

Swift might have been our great poet of the early eighteenth century had he not looked on St. Patrick's as a kennel and Ireland as a cage. 'I have not fingers enough to count the great Ministers that were my friends and that are gone', he said in Yeats' phrase, and, denied great office in England, he tore at the bars in Dublin satirizing that which he might have served. That he should become to the Irish people the heroic Drapier is as ironic in its way as that Yeats, the friend of John O'Leary, should write in old age songs for an abortive Fascist movement.

When in 1745 the Dean died, Oliver Goldsmith was a

youth of seventeen, and had they met the young Goldsmith would have shrunk under Swift's fierce stare. A gentle person, a kindly friend, not even a very bitter enemy, Goldsmith wrote and talked superficially for much of his life, but wrote three works which have survived the work of some of his more brilliant contemporaries. 'The Deserted Village' is a long poem, too long by modern standards, yet if one is to be true to the poet's intent where is it to be cut? In even the dullest passages there are fine lines, and it may be that a later age would deprecate our setting our taste above that of Dr. Johnson, who added the final resounding quatrain to his friend's lament.

Thomas Moore brought in the nineteenth century with a smile and a tear, though tears through that century were more common in verse than smiles. Moore was a brilliant technician who, happily for his fortunes, discovered the Bunting, Petrie, and Holden collections of Irish music, and to the tunes he found there wrote sad lyrics that charmed the age. He had been a friend of Robert Emmet, the leader who failed in the Rising of 1803, but who still lives through one enduring speech. In memory of that friendship Moore wrote a few songs that might have been considered faintly seditious. The English popularity of the Melodies is understandable since the words are impeccably English, set to tunes that were charmingly unfamiliar. Their Irish vogue is less easy to understand. The words derive from no Irish tradition and the tunes, though familiar, would have different associations for the hearers. In spite of, or perhaps because of their deep pessimism the Melodies appealed to a country sunk in apathy, famine, and ineffective revolution. Moore was quickly accepted as the Irish laureate and time has done little to dim the bays.

The first conscious attempt to write in English for an

Irish audience was unfortunate. In the early 1840's a group of young men calling themselves the Young Ireland Movement founded the *Nation* newspaper, edited by the ablest of the group, Thomas Davis. Here, written to Moore's Melodies and other popular Irish airs, appeared dozens of songs designed to rouse the people to action; they were seldom distinguished, but they had a success in their day even greater than Moore's and are still taught to ingenuous youth as poetry. However, in the pages of the *Nation* appeared the work of Mangan and the single ballad of John Kells Ingram, 'The Memory of the Dead', a work that haunted him in life and is his only memorial in death. He lived to become Vice-Provost of Trinity and came to distrust all radical politics, yet the song of his youth was a link between the Rising of 1798 and the rebels of later generations.

Mangan was the eccentric poet of nineteenth-century fiction come to fustian life. He was, says John Mitchel, 'an unearthly and ghostly figure, in a brown garment, the same to all appearance which lasted to the day of his death. The blanched hair was totally unkempt, the corpse-like features still as marble.' When he began to write translation was fashionable and for a time the papers of the day carried what he called translations from Persian, Hindustani, Romaic, and Coptic, though he knew little of those languages. Then, through the prose translations of the scholars O'Curry, O'Donovan, and O'Daly, he discovered Irish. It is possible that in this he was unlucky, for instead of becoming an original poet he was often content to be the medium for dead writers whose words he transmuted. Son of a bankrupt father, unlucky in love, he lived in penury and turned for solace to the popular literary anodynes of the time: opium, drink, and poetry, and when he died at the age of forty-six he had already become a legend, the poet of the might have been.

Mangan knew no Irish and made no attempt to learn it; Samuel Ferguson, his antithesis, translated felicitously and mellifluously, though with less respect for the original metre and rhythms. At his best he broke free from the vapid verse-forms of his day and reconstructed, as did Callanan and O'Curry, the country speech of the Irish poet.

Little original Irish verse of merit was written in English before Yeats, and though there were many nineteenth-century anthologies their contributions were largely gloomy obituary pieces or the swing of a shillelagh—a funerary landscape or Donnybrook Fair. Unknown to the writers of such verse was a submerged body of ballad-makers, many of them illiterate, who had a freshness and clarity of eye and frequently a sophisticated satire denied to the literate. Their work had evolved from the Irish language, though it had acquired English and Scottish overtones through the exchange of migratory labourers. Their ballads often attempted to import into English the assonance of Irish:

> Young men and tender maidens
> Throughout this Irish nation
> Who hear my lamentation
> I hope you'll pray for me,
> The truth I will unfold
> That my precious blood she sold
> In my grave I must lie cold,
> She's a dear maid to me.

There were, too, macaronic songs, with alternate lines in English and Irish:

> There's an ale-house near by
> *Agus béimuid go maidin ann*

> If you are satisfied
> *A ghrádh gheal mo chroidhe*
> Early next morning we'll send for the clergyman,
> *Agus béidhmid-ne ceangailt 'ngan-fhios d'on t-saoghal.*

This may be translated as:

> There's an ale-house nearby
> Where we'll stay till the morning-time
> If you are satisfied
> Bright love of my heart
> Early next morning we'll send for the clergyman
> And we'll be united unknown to the world.

There were lyrics, too, which might easily have come from England or Scotland and which frequently incorporated verses from the neighbouring countries:

> Were I at the Moss House where the birds do increase
> At the foot of Mount Leinster or some silent place
> By the streams of Bunclody where all pleasures do meet
> Then all I would ask is one kiss from you sweet.

> The cuckoo is a pretty bird it sings as it flies
> It brings us good tidings and tells us no lies
> It sucks the young birds' eggs to make its voice clear
> And the more it cries cuckoo the summer draws near.

There are hundreds, thousands of these anonymous songs and ballads of the seventeenth, eighteenth, and nineteenth centuries, scattered on broadsides and in little collections; at one time we considered including a selection, but we found it impossible to give adequate representation; they need a separate collection, with the music, for a folk-song without its music is a poor singer.

A few of the songs which we include have become 'folk': 'The Convict of Clonmel', 'Aghadoe', 'Páistín Fionn', 'The Memory of the Dead', and Yeats' 'Down by the Salley

Gardens', based on a folk-song 'Down by my Sally's Garden'. These are sung by people who never heard of their origin.

A question that will be asked is: What constitutes an Irish poet? In its simplest form the answer is easy, but there are exceptions. By our definition a poet may be Irish in three ways: by birth, by descent, by adoption. The majority of our poets are Irish by birth and there is no difficulty; some, such as Emily Brontë, Robert Graves, and Edward FitzGerald were born in England of Irish parentage. One, Sir Arnold Bax, had not, so far as we know, any Irish blood. His is a special case, since he came to live in Dublin before the war of 1914-18 and was friendly with the young revolutionary writers of the time—particularly Thomas MacDonagh, Padraic Pearse, and Joseph Plunkett. After the Rising of 1916, using the pseudonym 'Dermot O'Byrne' he wrote the 'Ballad of Dublin', which was suppressed by the British military authorities on its publication. We adopt him as an Irish poet, whether as 'Dermot O'Byrne' or Arnold Bax, Master of the King's Musick.

II

The nineteenth century, parsimonious of genius in Ireland, relented towards its close and gave us William Butler Yeats. That he was 'many-minded' his plays, his prose, his letters, even his life abundantly prove, but it is as a great poet that he will live. He learned, taught, pondered until words obeyed his will, and he made himself a master. Through fifty years of poetry he developed, outstripping his contemporaries, overtaking his successors, a wonder to the world and a delight to poets.

He was remarkable in many ways: in having a happy childhood, a wise and witty father, a brilliant family. Success came to him early, but not the dangerous gift of money-making. He knew, helped, or was helped by every great writer of his time from Shaw to Joyce and from Pound to Synge. His influence was great, but his wide and selective mind accepted influences throughout his life, from Tennyson and Morris and Blake in his youth to Auden and Spender in his splendid old age. Folk-tales and folk-songs he transmuted into something personal and strange; the mythology of Ireland, under his caress, softened and grew pale and turned to a Yeatsian dream of a faeryland that had little in common with Irish tradition—a Celtic Twilight that was his invention, and that died with him.

Unscholarly in youth, through his middle years he sent his imagination back to work among the book-stacks and found Hegel, Plotinus, Ovid, and Homer 'sages standing in God's holy fire' ready like his other 'singing-masters' to teach him and inspire.

He was lucky in women, lucky that the tall and lovely woman of his dream remained his Phoenix so that, lacking physical consummation, his love turned not to hate, but to poetry. He was lucky in the women who helped him with money and hard work to found the Abbey Theatre, lucky at last in his wife, to whose charm was added the gift of automatic writing and mediumship which unlocked the door to the world of spirits, or of dream, or the unconscious.

Tall and handsome, he was fortunate in never being satisfied, in never accepting excellence as perfection. In a late poem he examined his conscience:

> Everything he wrote was read,
> After certain years he won
> Sufficient money for his need,
> Friends that have been friends indeed;
> '*What then?*' sang Plato's ghost. '*What then?*'

All his happier dreams came true—
A small house, wife, daughter, son,
Grounds where plum and cabbage grew,
Poets and Wits about him drew;
'What then?' sang Plato's ghost. 'What then?'

'The work is done,' grown old he thought,
'According to my boyish plan;
Let the fools rave, I swerved at naught,
Something to perfection brought;'
But louder sang that ghost. 'What then?'

Yeats has pillaged the dictionary and laid waste for generations of poets unborn whole pages of epithets which have become Yeatsian by his use: 'rook-delighting heaven', 'a pearl-pale hand', 'the laborious stair', 'Quattrocento finger', 'high and solitary and most stern'; the examples could with ease be multiplied by random selection from the teeming pages.

Idiosyncratic in syntax and prosody, his poetry has that universality of image which makes it readily translatable, while remaining essentially the work of an Irish poet, which was his express intention.

．　　．　　．　　．　　．

Synge as a poet might well be forgotten today were it not for his fine plays; Joyce, too, might be unknown as a poet despite the charming lyrics of *Chamber Music* and *Pomes Pennyeach*. In each case we have included a number of their poems as well as some extracts from their larger works.

Of the poets after Yeats it may still be too early to speak. The young men who were executed in 1916 were 'coming into their force' but had already accomplished much, as had Ledwidge, who lamented them and who was himself

killed the following year. Seumas O'Sullivan had a delicate
and fragile talent; scholarly, strictly traditional, musical,
often a little remote from life, many of his poems have the
grace and charm of an eighteenth-century rectory. James
Stephens had wit and wisdom and a fine lyric gift, while
Padraic Colum, who outlived them all, wrote verse which
stemmed directly from the country songs of his youth and
wrote two of the most famous songs of Ireland; *The Old
Woman of the Roads*, which pursued him as relentlessly
throughout his life as *Innisfree* did Yeats, and *She Moved
through the Fair* in which he so successfully captured the
ballad method as to write a folk-song:

> My young love said to me, my mother won't mind
> And my father won't slight you for your lack of kind
> Then she stepped away from me, and this she did say,
> It will not be long love till our wedding-day.

Though he wrote successfully for over fifty years these
have been for too long almost his only well-known lyrics.
Joseph Campbell, too, had this dangerous gift, dangerous
because his better poetry is neglected, while his anthology
pieces appear in every school-book.

To the next generation belongs Austin Clarke, who in
his early poems turned back to medieval Ireland, to the
rich country of petty kings, great monasteries, jewelled
missals, learned ladies, and wandering scholars. Often bitter
and saturnine, he looks to distant times, situations, and
personages to symbolize his mistrust of the present. He,
like Yeats, preferred a *persona* through which to speak, so
that it is a Son of Learning, an abbot, a king, or a nun who
speaks his words. Taut, sometimes even to straining-point,
his technique is individual and impressive, his images vivid
and memorable.

F. R. Higgins, born in the same year as Clarke, went to the same well but brought back different gifts. His poetry has a wild and passionate richness, a colour and a movement often denied to Clarke, a gallivanting ribaldry, a sensuousness, but he is lacking in the intellectual subtlety which makes so many of Clarke's poems cunning puzzles:

> So many flagpoles can be seen now
> Freeing the crowd, while crisscross keys,
> On yellow and white above the green,
> Treble the wards of nation,
> God only knows what treasury
> Uncrams to keep each city borough
> And thoroughfare in grace.

Here it is necessary for reader or critic to know that the 'Celebrations' with which the poem deals are the Dublin Eucharistic Congress of 1932, that the Papal colours are yellow and white, with crossed keys, while the Irish flag is green, white, and yellow.

Robert Graves is another 'many-minded' man, poet, novelist, mythologist, historian. To an original mind is wed fine technique, and their progeny is poetry.

Patrick Kavanagh, self-levitated from the 'stony grey soil of Monaghan', is the articulate voice of the inarticulate small farmer, the poet of commonplace beauty:

> Dandelions growing on headlands, showing
> Their unloved hearts to everyone.

In his earlier poems he depended almost entirely on the country background for his effect—he was the country boy in the big town remembering the country scene: the spraying of the potatoes, the ploughing, the harvest, trees, and meadows. His verse was simple and direct. With the years he became more introspective and using the same country symbols expressed a more complex emotion. His long poem *The Great Hunger*, in which through the person of an old, repressed small-farmer who had 'made a field his bride', he showed the intellectual, emotional, and economic starvation of rural Ireland is unfortunately too long for inclusion here. It is filled with the deceptive quiet of the country, the inhibitions hidden under the apparent calm, the obsession with the land, the unacknowledged unhappiness, the little triumphs at cards, or being chosen to take the Church collection, the sudden beauty in the midst of squalor:

> No worry on Maguire's mind this day
> Except that he forgot to bring his matches . . .
> 'Hop back there Polly, hoy back, woa, wae,'
> From every second hill a neighbour watches
> With all the sharpened interest of rivalry.
> Yet sometimes when the sun comes through a gap
> These men know God the Father in a tree:
> The Holy Spirit is the rising sap,
> And Christ will be the green leaves that will come
> At Easter from the sealed and guarded tomb.

The contrast between the flat, prose-like lines and the sudden dart of beauty is typical of his work.

Because they were largely educated abroad and have lived there for so long Louis MacNeice and Cecil Day-Lewis are not often thought of as Irish poets. Of the two, Mac-Neice is the more obviously of Irish origin, his language has often the colour and the too-easy eloquence of his country, and often, as in the sequence of poems he wrote at the beginning of the Second World War, he turned to Ireland for his subjects. A writer of great lyric beauty and magnificent technique, Day-Lewis has little nostalgia for his

country, and, unlike W. R. Rodgers, seldom turns home for
a theme.

Rodgers, who had taken little interest in poetry until he
was nearly thirty, is a poet of many influences who has
succeeded in achieving a personal idiom; he stems from the
metaphysical poets of the seventeenth century on the one
side and from the school of Auden and Spender on the
other, and Gerard Manley Hopkins had a say in his educa-
tion. He assimilated his influences and what he has to say is
original and originally expressed. His words often tumble
over each other in their eagerness to be born; they rush
across the page in long lines, filled with radical metaphors
and similes.

Though most of the Irish poets under fifty know at least
some Irish, few of them have shown so much evidence oι
this as Robert Farren and Padraic Fallon, Farren deliberately
attempting to reproduce the Irish mode in English, and
Fallon writing in the racy and colourful idiom of his
native Connacht. Their elders, Patrick MacDonogh, Monk
Gibbon, Geoffrey Taylor, and Bryan Guinness, belong to
a different tradition and write almost as though they spoke
a different language.

What then is the authentic language, the authentic voice
of Ireland in verse? It is probably impossible to give an
adequate definition which would cover all cases.

Over the past fifty years it is the voice of Yeats, of
Joseph Campbell, of F. R. Higgins, Austin Clarke, Padraic
Colum, Padraic Fallon, Robert Farren. It need not be a trick
or a fashion, but a technique which each poet must evolve
for himself. Though each of these poets has the recognizably
Irish quality, it is almost all they have in common.

Even in this Irish voice there are many inflexions—there
are those who write out of that tradition of the countryside

which was introduced into Irish literature by Synge and Lady Gregory, and Yeats. These often clothe thought that is commonplace enough in language which is, in effect, a translation of Irish, and by mere novelty of language achieve an unjustified effect; while others write in language that is expressive, mobile, and subtle and follows the older tradition of Irish court poetry. But to demand a recognizably Irish voice as a rigid test of Irish poetry would be absurd, and would exclude many fine poets. A poet speaks the language he must and that which best conveys his thought.

DONAGH MacDONAGH

CONTENTS

CONTENTS

CONTENTS

CONTENTS

CONTENTS

CONTENTS

CONTENTS

CONTENTS

CONTENTS

CONTENTS

CONTENTS

CONTENTS

CONTENTS

CONTENTS

LUKE WADDING

1588–1657

1 *Christmas Day is Come*

CHRISTMAS Day is come; let's all prepare for mirth,
  Which fills the heav'ns and earth at this amazing birth.
Through both the joyous angels in strife and hurry fly,
  With glory and hosannas; 'All Holy' do they cry,
In heaven the Church triumphant adores with all her choirs,
  The militant on earth with humble faith admires.

But why should we rejoice? Should we not rather mourn
  To see the Hope of Nations thus in a stable born?
Where are His crown and sceptre, where is His throne
    sublime,
  Where is His train majestic that should the stars outshine?
Is there not sumptuous palace nor any inn at all
  To lodge His heav'nly mother but in a filthy stall?

NAHUM TATE

1652–1715

2 *While Shepherds Watched Their Flocks by Night*

WHILE shepherds watched their flocks by night,
    All seated on the ground,
The angel of the Lord came down,
    And glory shone around.

'Fear not,' said he, for mighty dread
    Had seized their troubled mind;
'Glad tidings of great joy I bring
    To you and all mankind.

'To you, in David's town, this day
    Is born of David's line,
The Saviour, who is Christ the Lord,
    And this shall be the sign:

'The heavenly babe you there shall find
    To human view displayed,
All meanly wrapped in swaddling bands,
    And in a manger laid.'

Thus spake the seraph; and forthwith
    Appeared a shining throng
Of angels, praising God, who thus
    Addressed their joyful song:

'All glory be to God on high,
    And to the earth be peace;
Good will henceforth from Heaven to men
    Begin and never cease.'

JONATHAN SWIFT

1667–1745

3   *Mrs. Frances Harris's Petition*

To their Excellencies, the Lord Justices of Ireland,
The humble petition of Frances Harris,
Who must starve and die a maid if it miscarries;

Humbly sheweth, that I went to warm myself in Lady
Betty's chamber because I was cold;
And I had in a purse seven pounds, four shillings, and six-
pence (besides farthings) in money and gold;
So, because I had been buying things for my lady last night,
I was resolved to tell my money, to see if it was right.
Now, you must know, because my trunk has a very bad lock,
Therefore all the money I have, which, God knows, is a
very small stock,
I keep in my pocket, ty'd about my middle, next my smock.
So when I went to put up my purse, as God would have it,
my smock was unript,
And instead of putting it into my pocket, down it slipt;
Then the bell rung, and I went down to put my lady to bed;
And, God knows I thought my money was as safe as my
maidenhead.
So, when I came up again, I found my pocket feel very
light;
But when I search'd, and missed my purse, Lord! I thought
I should have sunk outright.
'Lord! Madam,' says Mary, 'how d'ye do?'—'Indeed,' says
I, 'never worse:
But, pray, Mary, can you tell me what I have done with my
purse?'
'Lord help me!' says Mary, 'I never stirr'd out of this place!'
'Nay,' said I, 'I had it in Lady Betty's chamber, that's a
plain case.'
So Mary got me to bed, and covered me up warm;
However, she stole away my garters, that I might do myself
no harm.
So I tumbled and toss'd all night, as you may very well
think,
But hardly ever set my eyes together, or slept a wink.

So I was a-dreamed, methought that I went and searched
    the folks round,
And in a corner of Mrs. Duke's box, ty'd in a rag, the
    money was found,
So next morning we told Whittle, and he fell a-swearing;
Then my Dame Wadgar came, and she, you know, is thick
    of hearing.
'Dame,' said I, as loud as I could bawl, 'do you know what
    a loss I have had?'
'Nay,' says she, 'my Lord Colway's folks are all very sad:
For my Lord Dromedary comes a-Tuesday without fail.'
'Pugh!' said I, 'But that's not the business that I ail.'
Says Carey, says he, 'I have been a servant this five and
    twenty years come spring,
And in all the places I lived I never heard of such a thing.'
'Yes,' says the steward, 'I remember when I was at my Lord
    Shrewsbury's,
Such a thing as this happn'd, but just about the time of
    gooseberries.'
So I went to the party suspected and I found her full of
    grief:
(Now you must know, of all the things in the world I hate
    a thief:)
However, I was resolved to bring the discourse slyly about:
'Mrs. Duke,' said I, 'here's an ugly accident has happened out:
'Tis not that I value the money three skips of a louse:
But the thing I stand upon is the credit of the house.
'Tis true, seven pounds, four shillings and sixpence makes a
    great hole in my wages:
Besides, as they say, service is no inheritance in these ages.
Now, Mrs. Duke, you know, and everybody understands,
That though 'tis hard to judge, yet money can't go without
    hands.'

'The *devil* take me!' said she, (blessing herself,) 'if ever I
    saw it!'
So she roar'd like a bedlam, as tho' I had call'd her all to
    naught.
So, you know, what could I say to her any more?
I e'en left her, and came away as wise as I was before.
Well: but then they would have had me gone to the cun-
    ning man:
'No,' said I, ''tis the same thing, the CHAPLAIN will be here
    anon.'
So the Chaplain came in. Now the servants say he is my
    sweetheart,
Because he's always in my chamber, and I always take his part.
So, as the *devil* would have it, before I was aware, out I
    blunder'd,
'*Parson*,' said I, 'can you cast a *nativity*, when a body's
    plunder'd?'
(Now you must know, he hates to be called *Parson* like the
    devil!)
'Truly,' says he, 'Mrs. Nab, it might become you to be more
    civil;
If your money be gone, as a learned *Divine* says, d'ye see,
You are no *text* for my handling; so take that from me:
I was never taken for a *Conjuror* before, I'd have you to
    know.'
'Lord!' said I, 'don't be angry, I am sure I never thought
    you so;
You know I honour the cloth, I design to be a Parson's wife;
I never took one in *your coat* for a conjuror in all my life.'
With that he twisted his girdle at me like a rope, as who
    should say,
'Now you may go hang yourself for me!' and so went
    away.

Well: I thought I should have swoon'd. 'Lord!' said I, 'what
    shall I do?

I have lost my money, and shall lose my true love too!'

Then my lord called me: 'Harry,' said my lord, 'don't cry;

I'll give thee something toward thy loss:' 'And,' says my
    lady, 'so will I.'

'Oh! but,' said I, 'what if, after all, the Chaplain won't
    come to?'

For that, he said (an't please your Excellencies), I must peti-
    tion you.

The premisses tenderly consider'd, I desire your Excel-
    lencies' protection,

And that I may have a share in next Sunday's Collection;

And, over and above, that I may have your Excellencies'
    letter

With an order for the Chaplain aforesaid, or instead of him
    a better:

And then your poor petitioner, both night and day

Or the Chaplain (for 'tis his *trade*,) as in duty bound, shall
    ever *pray*.

4   *Stella's Birthday*

    ALL travellers at first incline
    Where'er they see the fairest sign,
    And if they find the chambers neat,
    And like the liquor and the meat,
    Will call again, and recommend
    The Angel Inn to every friend.
    And though the painting grows decay'd,
    The house will never lose its trade:
    Nay, though the treach'rous tapster, Thomas,

Hangs a new Angel two doors from us,
As fine as daubers' hands can make it,
In hopes that strangers may mistake it,
We think it both a shame and sin
To quit the true old Angel Inn.
   Now this is Stella's case in fact,
An angel's face a little crack'd.
(Could poets or could painters fix
How angels look at thirty-six:)
This drew us in at first to find
In such a form an angel's mind;
And every virtue now supplies
The fainting rays of Stella's eyes.
See, at her levee crowding swains,
Whom Stella freely entertains
With breeding, humour, wit, and sense,
And puts them to so small expense;
Their minds so plentifully fills,
And makes such reasonable bills,
So little gets for what she gives,
We really wonder how she lives!
And had her stock been less, no doubt
She must have long ago run out.
   Then, who can think we'll quit the place,
When Doll hangs out a newer face?
Nail'd to her window full in sight
All Christian people to invite,
Or stop and light at Chloe's head,
With scraps and leavings to be fed?
   Then, Chloe, still go on to prate
Of thirty-six and thirty-eight;
Pursue your trade of scandal-picking,
Your hints that Stella is no chicken;

Your innuendoes, when you tell us,
That Stella loves to talk with fellows:
But let me warn you to believe
A truth, for which your soul should grieve;
That should you live to see the day,
When Stella's locks must all be gray,
When age must print a furrow'd trace
On every feature of her face;
Though you, and all your senseless tribe,
Could Art, or Time, or Nature bribe,
To make you look like Beauty's Queen,
And hold for ever at fifteen;
No bloom of youth, can ever blind
The cracks and wrinkles of your mind:
All men of sense will pass your door,
And crowd to Stella's at four-score.

(Written 1720–1)

5   From *Cadenus and Vanessa*

Cupid tho' all his Darts were lost,
Yet still resolv'd to spare no Cost;
He cou'dn't answer to his Fame
The Triumphs of that stubborn Dame,
A Nymph so hard to be subdu'd,
Who neither was Coquette nor Prude;
I find, says he, she wants a Doctor,
Both to adore her and instruct her;
I'll give her what she most admires,
Among those venerable Sires;
Cadenus is a Subject fit,
Grown old in Politicks and Wit;

Caress'd by Ministers of State,
Of half Mankind the Dread and Hate.
Whate'er Vexations Love attend,
She need no Rivals apprehend.
Her Sex with universal Voice
Must laugh at her capricious Choice.
Cadenus many things had writ,
Vanessa much esteem'd his wit,
And call'd for his Poetick Works;
Mean-time the Boy in secret lurks,
And while the Book was in her Hand
The Urchin from his private Stand
Took Aim and shot with all his Strength,
A Dart of such prodigious Length,
It pierc'd the feeble Volume thro'
And deep transfix'd her Bosom too.
Some Lines, more moving than the rest
Stuck to the Point that pierc'd her Breast.
And borne directly to her Heart,
With Pains unknown increas'd her Smart.

Vanessa, not in Years a Score,
Doats on a Gown of forty-four;
Imaginary Charms can find,
In Eyes with reading almost blind;
Cadenus now no more appears
Declin'd in Health, advanc'd in years,
She fancies Musick in his Tongue,
Nor further looks, but thinks him young.
What Mariner is not afraid,
To venture in a Ship decay'd?
What Planter will attempt to yoke
A Sapling to a falling Oak?

As Years increase she brighter shines,
Cadenus with each day declines,
And he must fall a Prey to Time,
While she is blooming in her Prime.

OLIVER GOLDSMITH

1728–1774

6   *The Deserted Village*

SWEET Auburn! loveliest village of the plain;
Where health and plenty cheered the labouring swain,
Where smiling spring its earliest visit paid,
And parting summer's lingering blooms delayed:
Dear lovely bowers of innocence and ease,
Seats of my youth, when every sport could please,
How often have I loitered o'er thy green,
Where humble happiness endeared each scene!
How often have I paused on every charm,
The sheltered cot, the cultivated farm,
The never-failing brook, the busy mill,
The decent church that topped the neighbouring hill,
The hawthorn bush, with seats beneath the shade,
For talking age and whispering lovers made!
How often have I blest the coming day,
When toil remitting lent its turn to play,
And all the village train, from labour free,
Led up their sports beneath the spreading tree,
While many a pastime circled in the shade,
The young contending as the old surveyed;
And many a gambol frolicked o'er the ground,
And sleights of art and feats of strength went round.

And still, as each repeated pleasure tired,
Succeeding sports the mirthful band inspired;
The dancing pair that simply sought renown,
By holding out to tire each other down;
The swain mistrustless of his smutted face,
While secret laughter tittered round the place;
The bashful virgin's side-long looks of love,
The matron's glance that would those looks reprove:
These were thy charms, sweet village! sports like these,
With sweet succession, taught even toil to please:
These round thy bowers their cheerful influence shed:
These were thy charms—but all these charms are fled.
  Sweet smiling village, loveliest of the lawn,
Thy sports are fled, and all thy charms withdrawn:
Amidst thy bowers the tyrant's hand is seen,
And desolation saddens all thy green:
One only master grasps the whole domain,
And half a tillage stints thy smiling plain.
No more thy glassy brook reflects the day,
But, choked with sedges, works its weedy way;
Along thy glades, a solitary guest,
The hollow sounding bittern guards its nest;
Amidst thy desert walks the lapwing flies,
And tires their echoes with unvaried cries;
Sunk are thy bowers in shapeless ruin all,
And the long grass o'er-tops the mouldering wall;
And trembling, shrinking from the spoiler's hand,
Far, far away thy children leave the land.

  Ill fares the land, to hastening ills a prey,
Where wealth accumulates, and men decay:
Princes and lords may flourish, or may fade;
A breath can make them, as a breath has made;

But a bold peasantry, their country's pride,
When once destroyed, can never be supplied.

A time there was, ere England's griefs began,
When every rood of ground maintained its man;
For him light labour spread her wholesome store,
Just gave what life required, but gave no more:
His best companions, innocence and health;
And his best riches, ignorance of wealth.

But times are altered; trade's unfeeling train
Usurp the land and dispossess the swain;
Along the lawn, where scattered hamlets rose,
Unwieldy wealth and cumbrous pomp repose,
And every want to opulence allied,
And every pang that folly pays to pride.
Those gentle hours that plenty bade to bloom,
Those calm desires that asked but little room,
Those healthful sports that graced the peaceful scene,
Lived in each look, and brightened all the green;
These, far departing, seek a kinder shore,
And rural mirth and manners are no more.

Sweet Auburn! parent of the blissful hour,
Thy glades forlorn confess the tyrant's power.
Here, as I take my solitary rounds
Amidst thy tangling walks and ruined grounds,
And, many a year elapsed, return to view
Where once the cottage stood, the hawthorn grew,
Remembrance wakes with all her busy train,
Swells at my breast, and turns the past to pain.

In all my wanderings round this world of care,
In all my griefs—and God has given my share

I still had hopes, my latest hours to crown,
Amidst these humble bowers to lay me down;
To husband out life's taper at the close,
And keep the flame from wasting by repose:
I still had hopes, for pride attends us still,
Amidst the swains to show my book-learned skill,
Around my fire an evening group to draw,
And tell of all I felt, and all I saw;
And, as an hare whom hounds and horns pursue,
Pants to the place from whence at first she flew,
I still had hopes, my long vexations past,
Here to return—and die at home at last.
O! blest retirement, friend to life's decline,
Retreats from care, that never must be mine,
How happy he who crowns in shades like these,
A youth of labor with an age of ease;
Who quits a world where strong temptations try,
And, since 'tis hard to combat, learns to fly!
For him no wretches, born to work and weep,
Explore the mine, or tempt the dangerous deep;
No surly porter stands in guilty state,
To spurn the imploring famine from the gate;
But on he moves to meet his latter end,
Angels around befriending Virtue's friend;
Bends to the grave with unperceived decay,
While resignation gently slopes the way;
And, all his prospects brightening to the last,
His heaven commences ere the world be past!

Sweet was the sound, when oft at evening's close
Up yonder hill the village murmur rose.
There, as I passed with careless steps and slow,
The mingling notes came softened from below;

The swain responsive as the milk-maid sung,
The sober herd that lowed to meet their young,
The noisy geese that gabbled o'er the pool,
The playful children just let loose from school,
The watch-dog's voice that bayed the whispering wind,
And the loud laugh that spoke the vacant mind—
These all in sweet confusion sought the shade,
And filled each pause the nightingale had made.
But now the sounds of population fail,
No cheerful murmurs fluctuate in the gale,
No busy steps the grass-grown foot-way tread,
For all the bloomy flush of life is fled.
All but yon widowed, solitary thing,
That feebly bends beside the plashy spring:
She, wretched matron, forced in age, for bread,
To strip the brook with mantling cresses spread,
To pick her wintry faggot from the thorn,
To seek her nightly shed, and weep 'til morn;
She only left of all the harmless train,
The sad historian of the pensive plain.

Near yonder copse, where once the garden smiled,
And still where many a garden flower grows wild;
There, where a few torn shrubs the place disclose,
The village preacher's modest mansion rose.
A man he was to all the country dear,
And passing rich with forty pounds a year;
Remote from towns he ran his godly race,
Nor e'er had changed, nor wished to change his place;
Unpracticed he to fawn, or seek for power,
By doctrines fashioned to the varying hour;
Far other aims his heart had learned to prize,
More skilled to raise the wretched than to rise.

His house was known to all the vagrant train;
He chid their wanderings but relieved their pain:
The long-remembered beggar was his guest,
Whose beard descending swept his aged breast;
The ruined spendthrift, now no longer proud,
Claimed kindred there, and had his claims allowed;
The broken soldier, kindly bade to stay,
Sat by the fire, and talked the night away,
Wept o'er his wounds or, tales of sorrow done,
Shouldered his crutch and showed how fields were won.
Pleased with his guests, the good man learned to glow,
And quite forgot their vices in their woe;
Careless their merits or their faults to scan
His pity gave ere charity began.

Thus to relieve the wretched was his pride,
And e'en his failings leaned to Virtue's side;
But in his duty prompt at every call,
He watched and wept, he prayed and felt for all;
And, as a bird each fond endearment tries
To tempt its new-fledged offspring to the skies,
He tried each art, reproved each dull delay,
Allured to brighter worlds, and led the way.

Beside the bed where parting life was laid,
And sorrow, guilt, and pain by turns dismayed,
The reverend champion stood. At his control
Despair and anguish fled the struggling soul;
Comfort came down the trembling wretch to raise,
And his last faltering accents whispered praise.

At church, with meek and unaffected grace,
His looks adorned the venerable place;

Truth from his lips prevailed with double sway,
And fools, who came to scoff, remained to pray.
The service past, around the pious man,
With steady zeal, each honest rustic ran;
Even children followed with endearing wile,
And plucked his gown to share the good man's smile.
His ready smile a parent's warmth exprest;
Their welfare pleased him, and their cares distrest:
To them his heart, his love, his griefs were given,
But all his serious thoughts had rest in heaven.
As some tall cliff that lifts its awful form,
Swells from the vale, and midway leaves the storm,
Though round its breast the rolling clouds are spread,
Eternal sunshine settles on its head.

　　Beside yon straggling fence that skirts the way,
With blossomed furze unprofitably gay,
There, in his noisy mansion, skilled to rule,
The village master taught his little school.
A man severe he was, and stern to view;
I knew him well, and every truant knew;
Well had the boding tremblers learned to trace
The day's disasters in his morning face;
Full well they laughed with counterfeited glee
At all his jokes, for many a joke had he;
Full well the busy whisper circling round
Conveyed the dismal tidings when he frowned.
Yet he was kind, or, if severe in aught,
The love he bore to learning was in fault;
The village all declared how much he knew:
'Twas certain he could write, and cipher too;
Lands he could measure, terms and tides presage,
And even the story ran that he could gauge;

In arguing, too, the parson owned his skill,
For, even though vanquished, he could argue still;
While words of learned length and thundering sound
Amazed the gazing rustics ranged around;
And still they gazed, and still the wonder grew,
That one small head could carry all he knew.

But past is all his fame. The very spot
Where many a time he triumphed, is forgot.
Near yonder thorn, that lifts its head on high,
Where once the sign-post caught the passing eye,
Low lies that house where nut-brown draughts inspired,
Where graybeard mirth and smiling toil retired,
Where village statesmen talked with looks profound,
And news much older than their ale went round.
Imagination fondly stoops to trace
The parlour splendours of that festive place:
The white-washed wall, the nicely sanded floor,
The varnished clock that clicked behind the door;
The chest contrived a double debt to pay,
A bed by night, a chest of drawers by day;
The pictures placed for ornament and use,
The twelve good rules, the royal game of goose;
The hearth, except when winter chilled the day,
With aspen boughs and flowers and fennel gay;
While broken tea-cups, wisely kept for show,
Ranged o'er the chimney, glistened in a row.

Vain transitory splendours! could not all
Reprieve the tottering mansion from its fall?
Obscure it sinks, nor shall it more impart
An hour's importance to the poor man's heart.
Thither no more the peasant shall repair
To sweet oblivion of his daily care;

No more the farmer's news, the barber's tale,
No more the woodman's ballad shall prevail;
No more the smith his dusky brow shall clear,
Relax his ponderous strength, and lean to hear:
The host himself no longer shall be found
Careful to see the mantling bliss go round;
Nor the coy maid, half willing to be prest,
Shall kiss the cup to pass it to the rest.

 Yes! let the rich deride, the proud disdain,
These simple blessings of the lowly train;
To me more dear, congenial to my heart,
One native charm, than all the gloss of art.
Spontaneous joys, where Nature has its play,
The soul adopts, and owns their first born sway;
Lightly they frolic o'er the vacant mind,
Unenvied, unmolested, unconfined.
But the long pomp, the midnight masquerade,
With all the freaks of wanton wealth arrayed—
In these, ere triflers half their wish obtain,
The toiling pleasure sickens into pain;
And, even while fashion's brightest arts decoy,
The heart distrusting asks if this be joy.

 Ye friends to truth, ye statesmen, who survey
The rich man's joy increase, the poor's decay,
'Tis yours to judge, how wide the limits stand
Between a splendid and a happy land.
Proud swells the tide with loads of freighted ore,
And shouting Folly hails them from her shore;
Hoards even beyond the miser's wish abound,
And rich men flock from all the world around.
Yet count our gains! This wealth is but a name
That leaves our useful products still the same.

Not so the loss. The man of wealth and pride
Takes up a space that many poor supplied;
Space for his lake, his park's extended bounds,
Space for his horses, equipage, and hounds:
The robe that wraps his limbs in silken sloth
Has robbed the neighbouring fields of half their growth;
His seat, where solitary sports are seen,
Indignant spurns the cottage from the green:
Around the world each needful product flies,
For all the luxuries the world supplies;
While thus the land adorned for pleasure all
In barren splendour feebly waits the fall.
As some fair female unadorned and plain,
Secure to please while youth confirms her reign,
Slights every borrowed charm that dress supplies,
Nor shares with art the triumph of her eyes;
But when those charms are past, for charms are frail,
When time advances, and when lovers fail,
She then shines forth, solicitous to bless,
In all the glaring impotence of dress.
Thus fares the land by luxury betrayed:
In nature's simplest charms at first arrayed,
But verging to decline, its splendors rise,
Its vistas strike, its palaces surprise;
While, scourged by famine from the smiling land
The mournful peasant leads his humble band,
And while he sinks, without one arm to save,
The country blooms—a garden and a grave.

Where then, ah! where shall poverty reside,
To 'scape the pressure of contiguous pride?
If to some common's fenceless limits strayed,
He drives his flock to pick the scanty blade,

Those fenceless fields the sons of wealth divide,
And even the bare-worn common is denied.

   If to the city sped—what waits him there?
To see profusion that he must not share;
To see ten thousand baneful arts combined
To pamper luxury, and thin mankind;
To see those joys the sons of pleasure know
Extorted from his fellow-creature's woe.
Here while the courtier glitters in brocade,
There the pale artist plies the sickly trade;
Here while the proud their long-drawn pomps display,
There the black gibbet glooms beside the way.
The dome where Pleasure holds her midnight reign,
Here, richly decked, admits the gorgeous train:
Tumultuous grandeur crowds the blazing square,
The rattling chariots clash, the torches glare.
Sure scenes like these no troubles e'er annoy!
Sure these denote one universal joy!
Are these thy serious thoughts?—Ah, turn thine eyes
Where the poor houseless shivering female lies.
She once, perhaps, in village plenty blest,
Has wept at tales of innocence distrest;
Her modest looks the cottage might adorn,
Sweet as the primrose peeps beneath the thorn;
Now lost to all; her friends, her virtue fled,
Near her betrayer's door she lays her head,
And, pinched with cold, and shrinking from the shower,
With heavy heart deplores that luckless hour,
When idly first, ambitious of the town,
She left her wheel and robes of country brown.

   Do thine, sweet Auburn, thine, the loveliest train,
Do thy fair tribes participate her pain?

Even now, perhaps, by cold and hunger led,
At proud men's doors they ask a little bread!
Ah, no! To distant climes, a dreary scene,
Where half the convex world intrudes between,
Through torrid tracts with fainting steps they go,
Where wild Altama murmurs to their woe.
Far different there from all that charmed before
The various terrors of that horrid shore;
Those blazing suns that dart a downward ray,
And fiercely shed intolerable day;
Those matted woods, where birds forget to sing,
But silent bats in drowsy clusters cling;
Those poisonous fields with rank luxuriance crowned,
Where the dark scorpion gathers death around;
Where at each step the stranger fears to wake
The rattling terrors of the vengeful snake;
Where crouching tigers wait their hapless prey,
And savage men more murderous still than they;
While oft in whirls the mad tornado flies,
Mingling the ravaged landscape with the skies.
Far different these from every former scene,
The cooling brook, the grassy vested green,
The breezy covert of the warbling grove,
That only sheltered thefts of harmless love.

Good Heaven! what sorrows gloomed that parting day,
That called them from their native walks away:
When the poor exiles, every pleasure past,
Hung round the bowers, and fondly looked their last,
And took a long farewell, and wished in vain
For seats like these beyond the western main,
And shuddering still to face the distant deep,
Returned and wept, and still returned to weep.

The good old sire, the first prepared to go
To new found worlds, and wept for others' woe;
But for himself, in conscious virtue brave,
He only wished for worlds beyond the grave.
His lovely daughter, lovelier in her tears,
The fond companion of his helpless years,
Silent went next, neglectful of her charms,
And left a lover's for a father's arms.
With louder plaints the mother spoke her woes,
And blest the cot where every pleasure rose,
And kist her thoughtless babes with many a tear
And claspt them close, in sorrow doubly dear,
Whilst her fond husband strove to lend relief,
In all the silent manliness of grief.

　O luxury! thou curst by Heaven's decree,
How ill exchanged are things like these for thee!
How do thy potions, with insidious joy,
Diffuse their pleasure only to destroy!
Kingdoms by thee, to sickly greatness grown,
Boast of a florid vigor not their own.
At every draught more large and large they grow,
A bloated mass of rank, unwieldy woe;
Till sapped their strength, and every part unsound,
Down, down, they sink, and spread a ruin round.

　Even now the devastation is begun,
And half the business of destruction done;
Even now, methinks, as pondering here I stand,
I see the rural virtues leave the land.
Down where yon anchoring vessel spreads the sail
That idly waiting flaps with every gale,
Downward they move, a melancholy band,
Pass from the shore, and darken all the strand.

Contented toil, and hospitable care,
And kind connubial tenderness, are there;
And piety with wishes placed above,
And steady loyalty, and faithful love.
And thou, sweet Poetry, thou loveliest maid,
Still first to fly where sensual joys invade;
Unfit in these degenerate times of shame
To catch the heart, or strike for honest fame;
Dear charming nymph, neglected and decried,
My shame in crowds, my solitary pride;
Thou source of all my bliss, and all my woe,
That found'st me poor at first, and keep'st me so;
Thou guide by which the nobler arts excel,
Thou nurse of every virtue fare thee well!
Farewell, and oh! where'er thy voice be tried,
On Torno's cliff or Pambamarca's side,
Whether where equinoctial fervors glow,
Or winter wraps the polar world in snow,
Still let thy voice, prevailing over time,
Redress the rigours of the inclement clime;
Aid slighted truth with thy persuasive strain;
Teach erring man to spurn the rage of gain:
Teach him, that states of native strength possest,
Though very poor, may still be very blest;
That trade's proud empire hastes to swift decay,
As ocean sweeps the laboured mole away;
While self-dependent power can time defy,
As rocks resist the billows and the sky.

7 *Stanzas on Woman*

WHEN lovely woman stoops to folly,
   And finds too late that men betray,
What charm can soothe her melancholy,
   What art can wash her guilt away?

The only art her guilt to cover,
   To hide her shame from every eye,
To give repentance to her lover,
   And wring his bosom, is—to die.

JOHN O'KEEFE

1747–1833

8 *The Friar of Orders Gray*

I AM a friar of orders gray:
As down the valley I take my way,
   I pull not blackberry, haw, or hip,
   Good store of venison does fill my scrip:
   My long bead-roll I merrily chaunt,
   Where'er I walk, no money I want;
And why I'm so plump the reason I'll tell
Who leads a good life is sure to live well.
         What baron or squire
         Or knight of the shire
   Lives half so well as a holy friar!

After supper, of heaven I dream,
But that is fat pullet and clouted cream.
      Myself, by denial, I mortify
      With a dainty bit of a warden pie:

I'm clothed in sackcloth for my sin:
  With old sack wine I'm lined within:
A chirping cup is my matin song,
  And the vesper bell is my bowl's ding dong.
      What baron or squire
      Or knight of the shire
  Lives half so well as a holy friar!

RICHARD BRINSLEY SHERIDAN
1751–1816

9   *Let the Toast Pass*

HERE'S to the maiden of bashful fifteen,
  Here's to the widow of fifty;
Here's to the flaunting extravagant queen,
  And here's to the housewife that's thrifty.

Chorus
    Let the toast pass,
    Drink to the lass,
I'll warrant she'll prove an excuse for the glass.

Here's to the charmer whose dimples we prize,
  Now to the maid who has none, sir,
Here's to the girl with a pair of blue eyes,
  And here's to the nymph with but one, sir!
    Let the toast pass, &c.

Here's to the maid with a bosom of snow,
  And to her that's as brown as a berry;
Here's to the wife, with a face full of woe,
  And now to the damsel that's merry:
    Let the toast pass, &c.

For let 'em be clumsy, or let 'em be slim,
   Young or ancient, I care not a feather;
So fill the pint bumper quite up to the brim,
   And let us e'en toast them together:

Chorus

Let the toast pass,
Drink to the lass,
I'll warrant she'll prove an excuse for the glass.

WILLIAM DRENNAN
1754–1820

10   *The Wake of William Orr*

THERE our murdered brother lies;
Wake him not with woman's cries;
Mourn the way that manhood ought—
Sit in silent trance of thought.

Write his merits on your mind;
Morals pure and manners kind;
In his head, as on a hill,
Virtue placed her citadel.

Why cut off in palmy youth?
Truth he spoke, and acted truth.
'Countrymen, UNITE,' he cried,
And died for what our Saviour died.

God of peace and God of love!
Let it not Thy vengeance move—
Let it not Thy lightnings draw—
A nation guillotined by law.

WILLIAM DRENNAN

Hapless Nation, rent and torn,
Thou wert early taught to mourn;
Warfare for six hundred years!
Epoch marked with blood and tears!

Hunted thro' thy native grounds,
Or flung reward to human hounds,
Each one pulled and tore his share,
Heedless of thy deep despair.

Hapless Nation! hapless Land!
Heap of uncementing sand!
Crumbled by a foreign weight:
And by worse, domestic hate.

God of mercy! God of peace!
Make this mad confusion cease;
O'er the mental chaos move,
Through it SPEAK the light of love.

Monstrous and unhappy sight!
Brothers' blood will not unite;
Holy oil and holy water
Mix, and fill the world with slaughter.

Who is she with aspect wild?
The widowed mother with her child—
Child new stirring in the womb
Husband waiting for the tomb!

Angel of this sacred place,
Calm her soul and whisper peace—
Cord, or axe, or guillotine,
Make the sentence—not the sin.

WILLIAM DRENNAN

Here we watch our brother's sleep:
Watch with us, but do not weep:
Watch with us thro' dead of night—
But expect the morning light.

RICHARD ALFRED MILLIKEN

1767–1815

11   *The Groves of Blarney*

THE groves of Blarney
They look so charming,
Down by the purling
      Of sweet, silent brooks,
Being banked with posies
That spontaneous grow there,
Planted in order
      By the sweet 'Rock Close'.
'Tis there the daisy
And the sweet carnation,
The blooming pink
      And the rose so fair,
The daffydowndilly,
Likewise the lily,
All flowers that scent
      The sweet, fragrant air.

'Tis Lady Jeffers
That owns this station;
Like Alexander
      Or Queen Helen fair

There's no commander
In all the nation,
For emulation,
 Can with her compare.
Such walls surround her,
That no nine-pounder
Could dare to plunder
 Her place of strength;
But Oliver Cromwell
Her he did pommell,
And made a breach
 In her battlement.

There's gravel walks there
For speculation
And conversation
 In sweet solitude.
'Tis there the lover
May hear the dove, or
The gentle plover
 In the afternoon;
And if a lady
Would be so engaging
As to walk alone in
 Those shady bowers,
'Tis there the courtier
He may transport her
Into some fort, or
 All underground.

For 'tis there's a cave where
No daylight enters,
But cats and badgers
 Are for ever bred;

Being mossed by nature,
That makes it sweeter
Than a coach-and six or
    A feather bed.
'Tis there the lake is,
Well stored with perches,
And comely eels in
    The verdant mud;
Besides the leeches,
And groves of beeches,
Standing in order
    For to guard the flood.

There's statues gracing
This noble place in—
All heathen gods
    And nymphs so fair;
Bold Neptune, Plutarch,
And Nicodemus,
All standing naked
    In the open air!
So now to finish
This brave narration,
Which my poor genii
    Could not entwine;
But were I Homer,
Or Nebuchadnezzar,
'Tis in every feature
    I would make it shine.

THOMAS MOORE

1779–1852

12   *Child's Song*

I HAVE a garden of my own,
   Shining with flowers of every hue;
I loved it dearly while alone,
   But I shall love it more with you:
And there the golden bees shall come,
   In summer time at break of morn,
And wake us with their busy hum
   Around the Siha's fragrant thorn.

I have a fawn from Aden's land,
   On leafy buds and berries nurst;
And you shall feed him from your hand,
   Though he may start with fear at first.
And I will lead you where he lies
   For shelter from the noon-tide heat;
And you may touch his sleeping eyes
   And feel his little silv'ry feet.

13   *Echo*

HOW sweet the answer Echo makes
   To music at night,
When, roused by lute or horn, she wakes,
And, far away, o'er lawns and lakes,
   Goes answering light.

Yet Love hath echoes truer far,
   And far more sweet,
Than e'er beneath the moonlight's star,
Or horn or lute, or soft guitar,
   The songs repeat.

'Tis when the sigh, in youth sincere,
   And only then,—
The sigh that's breathed for one to hear,
Is by that one, that only dear,
   Breathed back again

14   *The Harp that once through Tara's
Halls*

THE harp that once through Tara's halls
   The soul of music shed,
Now hangs as mute on Tara's walls
   As if that soul were fled.
So sleeps the pride of former days,
   So glory's thrill is o'er,
And hearts, that once beat high for praise,
   Now feel that pulse no more.

No more to chiefs and ladies bright
   The harp of Tara swells;
The chord alone, that breaks at night,
   Its tale of ruin tells.
Thus freedom now so seldom wakes,
   The only throb she gives,
Is when some heart indignant breaks,
   To show that still she lives.

15 *At the Mid Hour of Night*

AT the mid hour of night, when stars are weeping, I fly
To the lone vale we loved, when life shone warm in thine
    eye;
And I think oft, if spirits can steal from the regions of air
To revisit past scenes of delight, thou wilt come to me there
And tell me our love is remembered, even in the sky!

Then I sing the wild song 'twas once such pleasure to hear!
When our voices, commingling, breathed like one on the
    ear;
And as Echo far off through the vale my sad orison rolls,
I think, Oh my love! 'tis thy voice from the Kingdom of
    Souls
Faintly answering still the notes that once were so dear.

16 *Has Sorrow Thy Young Days
Shaded?*

HAS sorrow thy young days shaded,
    As clouds o'er the morning fleet?
Too fast have those young days faded,
    That, even in sorrow, were sweet?
Does Time with his cold wing wither
    Each feeling that once was dear?
Then, child of misfortune, come hither,
    I'll weep with thee, tear for tear.

Has Hope, like the bird in the story,
    That flitted from tree to tree
With the talisman's glittering glory—
    Has Hope been that bird to thee?

On branch after branch alighting,
　The gem did she still display,
And, when nearest and most inviting,
　Then waft the fair gem away?

If thus the young hours have fleeted,
　When sorrow itself looked bright;
If thus the fair hope hath cheated,
　That led thee along so light;
If thus the cold world now wither
　Each feeling that once was dear:—
Come, child of misfortune, come hither,
　I'll weep with thee, tear for tear.

17　　　　*Oft, in the Stilly Night*

OFT, in the stilly night,
　Ere Slumber's chain has bound me,
Fond Memory brings the light
　Of other days around me;
　　The smiles, the tears
　　Of boyhood's years,
　The words of love then spoken;
　　The eyes that shone,
　　Now dimm'd and gone,
　The cheerful hearts now broken!
Thus, in the stilly night,
　Ere Slumber's chain has bound me,
Sad Memory brings the light
　Of other days around me.

When I remember all
   The friends, so link'd together,
I've seen around me fall
   Like leaves in wintry weather;
     I feel like one
     Who treads alone
   Some banquet-hall deserted,
     Whose lights are fled,
     Whose garlands dead,
   And all but he departed!
Thus, in the stilly night,
   Ere Slumber's chain has bound me,
Sad Memory brings the light
   Of other days around me.

18   *I Saw from the Beach*

I SAW from the beach, when the morning was shining,
   A bark o'er the waters move gloriously on;
I came when the sun from that beach was declining,
   The bark was still there, but the waters were gone.

And such is the fate of our life's early promise,
   So passing the spring-tide of joy we have known;
Each wave, that we danc'd on at morning, ebbs from us,
   And leaves us, at eve, on the bleak shore alone.

Ne'er tell me of glories, serenely adorning
   The close of our day, the calm eve of our night;—
Give me back, give me back the wild freshness of Morning,
   Her clouds and her tears are worth Evening's best light.

19   *All that's Bright must Fade*

ALL that's bright must fade,
The brightest still the fleetest;
All that's sweet was made
But to be lost when sweetest!

Stars that shine and fall;
The flower that drops in springing;
These, alas! are types of all
To which our hearts are clinging.

All that's bright must fade,
The brightest still the fleetest;
All that's sweet was made
But to be lost when sweetest.

Who would seek or prize
Delights that end in aching?
Who would trust to ties
That every hour are breaking?

Better far to be
In utter darkness lying,
Than to be blessed with light and see
That light forever flying.

All that's bright must fade,
The brightest still the fleetest;
All that's sweet was made
But to be lost when sweetest.

EATON STANNARD BARRETT

1786–1820

Woman

NOT she with traitorous kiss her Saviour stung,
Not she denied Him with unholy tongue;
She, while apostles shrank, could dangers brave,
Last at the cross and earliest at the grave.

CHARLES WOLFE

1791–1823

The Burial of Sir John Moore

NOT a drum was heard, not a funeral note,
  As his corse to the ramparts we hurried;
Not a soldier discharged his farewell shot
  O'er the grave where our hero we buried.

We buried him darkly, at dead of night,
  The sods with our bayonets turning,
By the struggling moonbeam's misty light,
  And the lantern dimly burning.

No useless coffin enclosed his breast,
  Not in sheet nor in shroud we wound him;
But he lay like a warrior taking his rest,
  With his martial cloak around him.

Few and short were the prayers we said,
  And we spake not a word of sorrow;
But we steadfastly gazed on the face that was dead,
  And we bitterly thought of the morrow.

We thought as we hollowed his narrow bed,
  And smoothed down his lonely pillow,
That the foe and the stranger would tread o'er his head,
  And we far away on the billow!

Lightly they'll talk of the spirit that's gone,
  And o'er his cold ashes upbraid him,—
But little he'll reck if they let him sleep on
  In a grave where a Briton has laid him.

But half of our heavy task was done,
  When the clock struck the hour for retiring,
And we heard the distant and random gun
  That the foe was sullenly firing.

Slowly and sadly we laid him down,
  From the field of his fame fresh and gory;
We carved not a line, and we raised not a stone—
  But we left him alone in his glory!

GEORGE DARLEY

1795–1846

22   *Siren Chorus*

TROOP home to silent grots and caves,
  Troop home! and mimic as you go
The mournful winding of the waves
  Which to their dark abysses flow.

At this sweet hour all things beside
  In amorous pairs to covert creep,
The swans that brush the evening tide
  Homeward in snowy couples keep.

In his green den the murmuring seal
  Close by his sleek companion lies,
While singly we to bedward steal,
  And close in fruitless sleep our eyes.

In bowers of love men take their rest,
  In loveless bowers we sigh alone,
With bosom-friends are others blest,
  But we have none, but we have none!

23   *On the Death of a Recluse*

LOVE drooped when Beauty fled the bower
  And languid closed the day,
Wept every little flower
  And turned its head away.

The wind spoke with a fallen tongue,
  The green reed sighed amain,
And sable forests swung
  Rude melody again.

Wild caves rang deep and rocks grew cold,
  Whilst rivers wept by them,
All nature's death-bells tolled
  A requiem! a requiem!

'Mid roaring brooks and dark moss-vales,
  Where speechless Thought abides,
Still her sweet spirit dwells,
  That knew no world besides.

Her form the woodland still retains—
    Wound but a creeping flower,
Her very life-blood stains
    Thee, in a falling shower.

Touch but the stream, drink but the air,
    Her cheek, her breath is known;
Ravish that red rose there,
    And she is all thine own.

The Sea Ritual

24

PRAYER unsaid, and Mass unsung,
Deadman's dirge must still be rung:
    Dingle-dong, the dead-bells sound!
    Mermen chant his dirge around!

Wash him bloodless, smooth him fair,
Stretch his limbs, and sleek his hair:
    Dingle-dong, the dead-bells go!
    Mermen swing them to and fro!

In the wormless sand shall he
Feast for no foul glutton be:
    Dingle-dong, the dead-bells chime!
    Mermen keep the tone and time!

We must with a tombstone brave
Shut the shark out from his grave:
    Dingle-dong, the dead-bells toll!
    Mermen dirgers ring his knoll!

Such a slab will we lay o'er him
All the dead shall rise before him!
    Dingle-dong, the dead-bells boom!
    Mermen lay him in his tomb!

J. J. CALLANAN

1795–1829

(*Translations from the Irish*)

25   *The Convict of Clonmel*

How hard is my fortune,
　And vain my repining!
The strong rope of fate
　For this young neck is twining!
My strength is departed,
　My cheeks sunk and sallow,
While I languish in chains
　In the jail of Clonmala.

No boy of the village
　Was ever yet milder;
I'd play with a child
　And my sport would be wilder;
I'd dance without tiring
　From morning till even,
And the goal-ball I'd strike
　To the lightning of heaven

At my bed-foot decaying,
　My hurl-bat is lying;
Through the boys of the village
　My goal-ball is flying;
My horse 'mong the neighbors
　Neglected may fallow,
While I pine in my chains
　In the jail of Clonmala.

Next Sunday the patron
   At home will be keeping,
And the young active hurlers
   The field will be sweeping;
With the dance of fair maidens
   The evening they'll hallow,
While this heart once so gay
   Shall be cold in Clonmala.

26   *The Outlaw of Loch Lene*

OH, many a day have I made good ale in the glen,
That came not of stream, or malt, like the brewing of men;
My bed was the ground; my roof the greenwood above,
And the wealth that I sought—one far kind glance from my
    love.

Alas! on that night when the horses I drove from the field,
That I was not near, from terror my angel to shield!
She stretched forth her arms—her mantle she flung to the
    wind,
And swam o'er Loch Lene, her outlawed lover to find.

Oh, would that a freezing, sleet-winged tempest did sweep,
And I and my love were alone, far off on the deep!
I'd ask not a ship, or a bark, or pinnace to save—
With her hand round my waist, I'd fear not the wind or the
    wave.

'Tis down by the lake where the wild tree fringes its sides,
The maid of my heart, the fair one of heaven resides:
I think, as at eve she wanders its mazes along,
The birds go to sleep by the sweet wild twist of her song.

EUGENE O'CURRY

1796–1862

27 *Do You Remember that Night?*

(From the Irish)

Do you remember that night
When you were at the window,
With neither hat nor gloves
Nor coat to shelter you?
I reached out my hand to you,
And you ardently grasped it;
I remained to converse with you
Until the lark began to sing.

Do you remember that night
That you and I were
At the foot of the rowan tree,
And the night drifting snow?
Your head on my breast,
And your pipe sweetly playing?
Little thought I that night
That our love ties would loosen!

Beloved of my inmost heart,
Come some night and soon,
When my people are at rest,
That we may talk together.
My arms shall encircle you
While I relate my sad tale,
That your soft, pleasant converse
Hath deprived me of heaven.

43

The fire is unraked,
The light unextinguished,
The key under the door,
Do you softly draw it.
My mother is asleep,
But I am wide awake;
My fortune in my hand,
I am ready to go with you.

JAMES CLARENCE MANGAN
1803–1849

28   *The Nameless One*

ROLL forth, my song, like the rushing river
   That sweeps along to the mighty sea;
God will inspire me while I deliver
      My soul of thee!

Tell thou the world, when my bones lie whitening
   Amid the lost homes of youth and eld,
That there was once one whose veins ran lightning
      No eye beheld.

Tell how his boyhood was one drear night-hour,
   How shone for *him*, through his griefs and gloom,
No star of all Heaven sends to light our
      Path to the tomb.

Roll on, my song, and to after ages
   Tell how, disdaining all earth can give,
He would have taught men, from Wisdom's pages,
      The way to live.

And tell how trampled, derided, hated,
   And worn by weakness, disease, and wrong,
He fled for shelter to God, who mated
          His soul with song—

With song which alway, sublime or vapid,
   Flowed like a rill in the morning-beam,
Perchance not deep, but intense and rapid—
          A mountain stream.

Tell how this Nameless, condemned for years long
   To herd with demons from Hell beneath,
Saw things that made him, with groans and tears, long
         For even death.

Go on to tell how, with genius wasted,
   Betrayed in friendship, befooled in love,
With spirit shipwrecked, and young hopes blasted,
         He still, still strove

Till, spent with toil, dreeing death for others,
   And some whose hands should have wrought for *him;*
(If children live not for sires and mothers),
         His mind grew dim.

And he fell far through that pit abysmal,
   The gulf and grave of Maginn and Burns,
And pawned his soul for the devil's dismal
         Stock of returns.

But yet redeemed it in days of darkness,
   And shapes and signs of the final wrath,
When death, in hideous and ghastly starkness,
         Stood on his path.

And tell how, now, amid wreck and sorrow,
 And want, and sickness, and houseless nights,
He bides in calmness the silent morrow,
  That no ray lights.

And lives he still, then? Yes! Old and hoary
 At thirty-nine, from despair and woe,
He lives, enduring what future story
  Will never know.

Him grant a grave to, ye pitying noble,
 Deep in your bosoms! There let him dwell!
He, too, had tears for all souls in trouble,
  Here and in Hell.

29   *Ode to the Maguire*

(*From the Irish*)

WHERE is my Chief, my Master, this bleak night, *mavrone!*[1]
O, cold, cold, miserably cold is this bleak night for Hugh,
Its showery, arrowy, speary sleet pierceth one through and
  through,
Pierceth one to the very bone!

Rolls real thunder? Or, was that red, livid light
Only a meteor? I scarce know; but through the midnight
  dim
The pitiless ice-wind streams. Except the hate that perse-
  cutes *him*
Nothing hath crueller venomy might.

[1] *mo bhrón*: my sorrow.

An awful, a tremendous night is this, meseems!
The flood-gates of the rivers of heaven, I think, have been
    burst wide—
Down from the overcharged clouds, like unto headlong
    ocean's tide,
Descends grey rain in roaring streams.

Though he were even a wolf ranging the round green
    woods,
Though he were even a pleasant salmon in the unchainable
    sea,
Though he were a wild mountain eagle, he could scarce
    bear, he,
This sharp, sore sleet, these howling floods.

O, mournful is my soul this night for Hugh Maguire!
Darkly, as in a dream he strays! Before him and behind
Triumphs the tyrannous anger of the wounding wind,
The wounding wind, that burns as fire!

It is my bitter grief—it cuts me to the heart—
That in the country of Clan Darry this should be his
    fate!
O, woe is me, where is he? Wandering, houseless,
    desolate,
Alone, without a guide or chart!

Medreams I see just now his face, the strawberry-bright,
Uplifted to the blackened heavens, while the tempestuous
    winds
Blow fiercely over and around him, and the smiting sleet-
    shower blinds
The hero of Galang to-night!

Large, large affliction unto me and mine it is,
That one of his majestic bearing, his fair, stately form,
Should thus be tortured and o'erborne—that this unsparing
    storm
Should wreck its wrath on head like his!

That his great hand, so oft the avenger of the oppressed,
Should this chill, churlish night, perchance, be paralyzed by
    frost—
While through some icicle-hung thicket—as one lorn and
    lost—
He walks and wanders without rest.

The tempest-driven torrent deluges the mead,
It overflows the low banks of the rivulets and ponds—
The lawns and pasture-grounds lie locked in icy bonds
So that the cattle cannot feed.

The pale bright margins of the streams are seen by none,
Rushes and sweeps along the untamable flood on every
    side—
It penetrates and fills the cottagers' dwellings far and
    wide—
Water and land are blent in one.

Through some dark woods, 'mid bones of monsters, Hugh
    now strays,
As he confronts the storm with anguished heart, but manly
    brow—
O! what a sword-wound to the tender heart of his were
    now
A backward glance at peaceful days!

But other thoughts are his—thoughts that can still inspire
With joy and an onward-bounding hope the bosom of
  MacNee—
Thoughts of his warriors charging like bright billows of the
  sea,
Borne on the wind's wings, flashing fire!

And though frost glaze to-night the clear dew of his eyes,
And white ice-gauntlets glove his noble fine fair fingers o'er,
A warm dress is to him that lightning-garb he ever wore,
The lightning of the soul, not skies.

Avran[1]

Hugh marched forth to the fight—I grieved to see him so
  depart;
And lo! to-night he wanders frozen, rain-drenched, sad,
  betrayed—
But the memory of the limewhite mansions his right hand hath
  laid
In ashes, warms the hero's heart!

30   *Gone in the Wind*

SOLOMON! where is thy throne? It is gone in the wind.
Babylon! where is thy might? It is gone in the wind.
Like the swift shadows of Noon, like the dreams of the
  Blind,
Vanish the glories and pomps of the earth in the wind.

---

[1] *amhrán*: song.

Man! canst thou build upon aught in the pride of thy mind?
Wisdom will teach thee that nothing can tarry behind;
Though there be thousand bright actions embalmed and
    enshrined,
Myriads and millions of brighter are snow in the wind.

Solomon! where is thy throne? It is gone in the wind.
Babylon! where is thy might? It is gone in the wind.
All that the genius of Man hath achieved or designed
Waits but its hour to be dealt with as dust by the wind.

Say, what is Pleasure? A phantom, a mask undefined.
Science? An almond, whereof we can pierce but the
    rind.
Honor and Affluence? Firmans that Fortune hath signed
Only to glitter and pass on the wings of the wind.

Solomon! where is thy throne? It is gone in the wind.
Babylon! where is thy might? It is gone in the wind.
Who is the Fortunate? He who in anguish hath pined!
He shall rejoice when his relics are dust in the wind!

Mortal! be careful with what thy best hopes are entwined;
Woe to the miners for Truth—where the Lampless have
    mined!
Woe to the seekers on earth for—what none ever find!
They and their trust shall be scattered like leaves on the
    wind.

Solomon! where is thy throne? It is gone in the wind.
Babylon! where is thy might? It is gone in the wind.
Happy in death are they only whose hearts have consigned
All Earth's affections and longings and cares to the wind.

Pity, thou, reader! the madness of poor Humankind,
Raving of Knowledge,—and Satan so busy to blind!
Raving of Glory,—like me,—for the garlands I bind
(Garlands of song) are but gathered, and—strewn in the
    wind!

Solomon! where is thy throne? It is gone in the wind.
Babylon, where is thy might? It is gone in the wind.
I, Abul-Namez, must rest; for my fire hath declined,
And I hear voices from Hades like bells on the wind!

31   *The Woman of Three Cows*

O WOMAN of Three Cows, *agra!*[1] don't let your tongue
    thus rattle!
Oh, don't be saucy, don't be stiff, because you may have
    cattle.
I have seen—and, here's my hand to you, I only say what's
    true—
A many a one with twice your stock not half so proud as
    you.

Good luck to you, don't scorn the poor, and don't be their
    despiser;
For worldly wealth soon melts away, and cheats the very
    miser;
And Death soon strips the proudest wreath from haughty
    human brows—
Then don't be stiff, and don't be proud, good Woman of
    Three Cows!

[1] *a ghrádh*: my love.

See where Momonia's heroes lie, proud Owen Mór's de-
    scendants,
'Tis they that won the glorious name, and had the grand
    attendants;
If *they* were forced to bow to Fate, as every mortal bows,
Can *you* be proud, can *you* be stiff, my Woman of Three
    Cows?

The brave sons of the Lord of Clare, they left the land to
    mourning;
Mavrone![1] for they were banished, with no hope of their
    returning.
Who knows in what abodes of want those youths were
    driven to house?
Yet *you* can give yourself these airs, O Woman of Three
    Cows.

O, think of Donnell of the Ships, the Chief whom nothing
    daunted,
See how he fell in distant Spain unchronicled, unchanted!
He sleeps, the great O'Sullivan, where thunder cannot
    rouse—
Then ask yourself, should *you* be proud, good Woman of
    Three Cows?

O'Ruark, Maguire, those souls of fire, whose names are
    shrined in story:
Think how their high achievements once made Erin's
    greatest glory.
Yet now their bones lie mouldering under weeds and
    cypress boughs—
And so, for all your pride, will yours, O Woman of Three
    Cows.

[1] *mo bhrón*: my sorrow.

Th' O'Carrolls, also, famed when fame was only for the
  boldest,
Rest in forgotten sepulchres with Erin's best and oldest;
Yet who so great as they of yore in battle or carouse?
Just think of that, and hide your head, good Woman of
  Three Cows.

Your neighbour's poor; and you, it seems, are big with vain
  ideas,
Because, forsooth, you've got three cows—one more, I see,
  than *she* has;
That tongue of yours wags more at times than charity
  allows;
But if you're strong, be merciful—great Woman of Three
  Cows.

Avran[1]

Now, there you go; you still, of course, keep up your
  scornful bearing,
And I'm too poor to hinder you; but, by the cloak I'm
  wearing,
If I had but *four* cows myself, even though you were my
  spouse,
I'd thwack you well, to cure your pride, my Woman of
  Three Cows.

32   *Farewell to Patrick Sarsfield*
        (*From the Irish*)

FAREWELL, O Patrick Sarsfield! May luck be on your path!
  Your camp is broken up—your work is marred for years—
But you go to kindle into flame the King of France's wrath,
  Though you leave sick Eire in tears.

[1] *amhrán*: song.

May the white sun and moon rain glory on your head,
   All hero as you are, and holy man of God!
To you the Saxons owe a many an hour of dread
   In the land you have often trod.

The Son of Mary guard you, and bless you to the end!
   'Tis altered is the time since your legions were astir,
When at Cullen you were hailed as the Conqueror and
     Friend,
   And you crossed narrow water near Birr.

I'll journey to the North, over mount, moor, and wave;
   'Twas there I first beheld, drawn up in file and line,
The brilliant Irish hosts—they were bravest of the brave,
   But, alas! they scorned to combine!

I saw the royal Boyne, when its billows flashed with blood.
   I fought at Grána Oge, where a thousand horsemen fell.
On the dark empurpled field of Aughrim, too, I stood,
   On the plain by Tubberdonny's Well.

To the heroes of Limerick, the City of the Fights,
   Be my best blessing borne on the wings of the air!
We had card-playing there by our camp-fires at night,
   And the Word of Life, too, and prayer.

But, for you, Londonderry, may Plague smite and slay
   Your people! May ruin desolate you stone by stone!
Through you a many a gallant youth lies coffinless today,
   With the winds for mourners alone!

I clomb the high hill on a fair summer noon,
   And saw the Saxon Muster, clad in armour blinding
     bright,
Oh, rage withheld my hand, or gunsman and dragoon
   Should have supped with Satan that night!

How many a noble soldier, how many a cavalier,
   Careered along this road seven fleeting weeks ago,
With silver-hilted sword, with matchlock and with spear,
   Who now, *mavrone*,[1] lieth low!

All hail to thee Ben Edir—But ah, on thy brow
   I see a limping soldier, who battled and who bled
Last year in the cause of the Stuart, though now
   The worthy is begging his bread!

And Diarmuid! oh Diarmuid! he perished in the strife—
   His head it was spiked on a halbert so high;
His colours they were trampled; he had no chance of life,
   If the Lord God Himself stood by.

But most, oh, my woe! I lament and lament
   For the ten valiant heroes who dwelt nigh the Nore,
And my three blessed brothers! They left me, and they went
   To the wars—and returned no more!

On the Bridge of the Boyne was our first overthrow;
   By Slaney the next, for we battled without rest:
The third was at Aughrim. Oh, Eire thy woe
   Is a sword in my bleeding breast!

O! the roof above our heads it was barbarously fired,
   While the black Orange guns blazed and bellowed
     around,
And as volley followed volley, Colonel Mitchel enquired
   Whether Lucan still stood his ground.

But O'Kelly still remains, to defy and to toil;
   He has memories that Hell won't permit him to forget,
And a sword that will make the blue blood flow like oil
   Upon many an Aughrim yet!

       [1] *mo bhrón*: my sorrow.

And I never shall believe that my Fatherland can fall
    With the Burkes, and the Decies, and the son of Royal
      James,
And Talbot the Captain, and *Sarsfield* above all,
    The beloved of damsels and dames.

33   *Dark Rosaleen*

                (*From the Irish*)

O, MY Dark Rosaleen,
    Do not sigh, do not weep!
The priests are on the ocean green,
    They march along the Deep.
There's wine from the royal Pope,
    Upon the ocean green;
And Spanish ale shall give you hope,
    My Dark Rosaleen!
    My own Rosaleen!
Shall glad your heart, shall give you hope,
Shall give you health, and help, and hope,
    My Dark Rosaleen!

Over hills, and through dales,
    Have I roamed for your sake;
All yesterday I sailed with sails
    On river and on lake.
The Erne, at its highest flood,
    I dashed across unseen,
For there was lightning in my blood,
    My Dark Rosaleen!
    My own Rosaleen!
Oh! there was lightning in my blood,
Red lightning lightened through my blood,
    My Dark Rosaleen!

All day long, in unrest,
　To and fro, do I move.
The very soul within my breast
　Is wasted for you, love!
The heart in my bosom faints
　To think of you, my Queen,
My life of life, my saint of saints,
　My Dark Rosaleen!
　My own Rosaleen!
To hear your sweet and sad complaints,
My life, my love, my saint of saints,
　My Dark Rosaleen!

Woe and pain, pain and woe,
　Are my lot, night and noon,
To see your bright face clouded so,
　Like to the mournful moon.
But yet will I rear your throne
　Again in golden sheen;
'Tis you shall reign, shall reign alone,
　My Dark Rosaleen!
　My own Rosaleen!
'Tis you shall have the golden throne,
'Tis you shall reign, and reign alone,
　My Dark Rosaleen!

Over dews, over sands,
　Will I fly, for your weal:
Your holy, delicate white hands
　Shall girdle me with steel.
At home in your emerald bowers,
　From morning's dawn till e'en,
You'll pray for me, my flower of flowers,
　My Dark Rosaleen!

My fond Rosaleen!
You'll think of me through daylight's hours,
My virgin flower, my flower of flowers,
   My Dark Rosaleen!

I could scale the blue air,
   I could plough the high hills,
Oh, I could kneel all night in prayer,
   To heal your many ills!
And one beamy smile from you
   Would float like light between
My toils and me, my own, my true,
   My Dark Rosaleen!
   My fond Rosaleen!
Would give me life and soul anew,
A second life, a soul anew,
   My dark Rosaleen!

O! the Erne shall run red
   With redundance of blood,
The earth shall rock beneath our tread,
   And flames wrap hill and wood,
And gun-peal, and slogan cry
   Wake many a glen serene,
Ere you shall fade, ere you shall die,
   My Dark Rosaleen!
   My own Rosaleen!
The Judgment Hour must first be nigh,
Ere you can fade, ere you can die,
   My Dark Rosaleen!

34

Kincora

(*From the Irish*)

OH, where Kincora! is Brian the Great?
And where is the beauty that once was thine?
Oh, where are the princes and nobles that sate
At the feast in thy halls, and drank the red wine?
          Where, oh, Kincora?

Oh, where, Kincora! are thy valorous lords?
Oh, whither, thou Hospitable! are they gone?
Oh, where are the Dalcassians of the Golden Swords?
And where are the warriors Brian led on?
          Where, oh, Kincora?

And where is Murrough, the descendant of kings—
The defeater of a hundred—the daringly brave—
Who set but slight store by jewels and rings—
Who swam down the torrent and laughed at its wave?
          Where, oh, Kincora?

And where is Donogh, King Brian's worthy son?
And where is Conaing, the Beautiful Chief?
And Kian, and Corc? Alas! they are gone—
They have left me this night alone with my grief,
          Left me, Kincora!

And where are the chiefs with whom Brian went forth,
The ne'er vanquished son of Erin the Brave,
The great King of Onaght, renowned for his worth,
And the hosts of Baskinn, from the western wave?
          Where, oh, Kincora?

Oh, where is Duvlann of the swift-footed Steeds?
And where is Kian, who was son of Molloy?
And where is King Lonergan, the fame of whose deeds
In the red battle-field no time can destroy?
           Where, oh, Kincora?

And where is that youth of majestic height,
The faith-keeping Prince of the Scots?—Even he,
As wide as his fame was, as great as was his might,
Was tributary, oh, Kincora, to thee!
           Thee, oh, Kincora!

They are gone, those heroes of royal birth,
Who plundered no churches, and broke no trust,
'Tis weary for me to be living on earth
When they, oh, Kincora, lie low in the dust!
           Low, oh, Kincora!

Oh, never again will Princes appear,
To rival the Dalcassians of the Cleaving Swords!
I can never dream of meeting afar or anear,
In the east or the west, such heroes and lords!
           Never, Kincora!

Oh, dear are the images my memory calls up
Of Brian Boru!—how he never would miss
To give me at the banquet the first bright cup!
Ah! why did he heap on me honour like this?
           Why, oh, Kincora?

I am Mac Liag, and my home is on the Lake;
Thither often, to that palace whose beauty is fled
Came Brian to ask me, and I went for his sake
Oh, my grief! that I should live, and Brian be dead!
           Dead, oh, Kincora!

GEORGE FOX

1809–1880

35   *The County of Mayo*
(*From the Irish*)

On the deck of Patrick Lynch's boat I sat in woeful plight,
Through my sighing all the weary day and weeping all the
 night.
Were it not that full of sorrow from my people forth I go,
By the blessed sun, 'tis royally I'd sing thy praise, Mayo.

When I dwelt at home in plenty, and my gold did much
 abound,
In the company of fair young maids the Spanish ale went
 round.
'Tis a bitter change from those gay days that now I'm forced
 to go,
And must leave my bones in Santa Cruz, far from my own
 Mayo.

They're altered girls in Irrul now; 'tis proud they're grown
 and high,
With their hair-bags and their top-knots—for I pass their
 buckles by;
But it's little now I heed their airs, for God will have it so,
That I must depart for foreign lands, and leave my sweet
 Mayo.

'Tis my grief that Patrick Loughlin is not Earl in Irrul still,
And that Brian Duff no longer rules as Lord upon the Hill;
And that Colonel Hugh MacGrady should be lying dead
 and low,
And I sailing, sailing swiftly from the county of Mayo.

EDWARD FITZGERALD

1809–1883

36 From *The Rubá'iyát of Omar Khayyám
of Naishápúr*

AWAKE! for Morning in the Bowl of Night
Has flung the Stone that puts the Stars to flight:
  And Lo! the Hunter of the East has caught
The Sultán's Turret in a Noose of Light.

Come, fill the Cup, and in the Fire of Spring
The Winter Garment of Repentance fling:
  The Bird of Time has but a little way
To fly—and Lo! the Bird is on the Wing.

A Book of Verses underneath the Bough,
A Jug of Wine, a Loaf of Bread—and Thou
  Beside me singing in the Wilderness—
O, Wilderness were Paradise enow!

Some for the Glories of This World; and some
Sigh for the Prophet's Paradise to come;
  Ah, take the Cash, and let the Credit go,
Nor heed the rumble of a distant Drum.

Think, in this batter'd Caravanserai
Whose Portals are alternate Night and Day,
  How Sultán after Sultán with his Pomp
Abode his destined Hour, and went his way.

They say the Lion and the Lizard keep
The Courts where Jamshyd gloried and drank deep:
  And Bahrám, that great Hunter—the Wild Ass
Stamps o'er his Head, but cannot break his Sleep.

I sometimes think that never blows so red
The Rose as where some buried Caesar bled;
   That every Hyacinth the Garden wears
Dropt in her Lap from some once lovely Head.

Ah, make the most of what we yet may spend,
Before we too into the Dust descend;
   Dust unto Dust, and under Dust to lie;
Sans Wine, sans Song, sans Singer, and—sans End!

SAMUEL FERGUSON
1810–1886

37   *Lament for the Death of Thomas Davis*

I WALKED through Ballinderry in the springtime,
   When the bud was on the tree,
And I said, in every fresh-ploughed field beholding
   The sowers striding free,
Scattering broadcast forth the corn in golden plenty,
   On the quick, seed-clasping soil,
'Even such this day, among the fresh-stirred hearts of Erin,
   Thomas Davis, is thy toil!'

I sat by Ballyshannon in the summer,
   And saw the salmon leap,
And I said, as I beheld the gallant creatures
   Spring glittering from the deep,
Through the spray and through the prone heaps striving
     onward
   To the calm clear streams above,
'So seekest thou thy native founts of freedom, Thomas
     Davis,
   In thy brightness of strength and love!'

I stood in Derrybawn in the autumn,
   I heard the eagle call,
With a clangorous cry of wrath and lamentation
   That filled the wide mountain hall,
O'er the bare, deserted place of his plundered eyrie,
   And I said, as he screamed and soared,
'So callest thou, thou wrathful-soaring Thomas Davis,
   For a nation's rights restored.'

And Alas! to think but now that thou art lying,
   Dear Davis, dead at thy mother's knee,
And I, no mother near, on my own sick-bed,
   That face on earth shall never see;
I may lie and try to feel that I am dreaming,
   I may lie and try to say, 'Thy Will be done'—
But a hundred such as I will never comfort Erin
   For the loss of that noble son.

Young husbandman of Erin's fruitful seed-time,
   In the fresh track of danger's plough!
Who will walk the heavy, toilsome, perilous furrow,
   Girt with freedom's seed-sheets now?
Who will vanish with the wholesome crop of knowledge,
   The flaunting weed and the bitter thorn,
Now that thou thyself art but a seed for hopeful planting
   Against the resurrection morn?

Young salmon of the flood-time of freedom
   That swells round Erin's shore,
Thou wilt leap against their loud, oppressive torrent
   Of bigotry and hate no more!
Drawn downward by their prone material instinct,
   Let them thunder on their rocks, and foam;
Thou hast leaped, aspiring soul, to founts beyond their raging,
   Where troubled waters never come.

But I grieve not, eagle of the empty eyrie,
   That thy wrathful cry is still,
And that the songs alone of peaceful mourners
   Are heard to-day on Erin's hill.
Better far if brothers' war be destined for us—
   God avert that horrid day, I pray!—
That ere our hands be stained with slaughter fratricidal,
   Thy warm heart should be cold in clay.

But my trust is strong in God who made us brothers,
   That He will not suffer these right hands,
Which thou hast joined in holier rites than wedlock,
   To draw opposing brands.
O many a tuneful tongue that thou madest vocal,
   Would lie cold and silent then,
And songless long once more should often-widowed Erin
   Mourn the loss of her brave young men.

O brave young men, my love, my pride, my promise,
   'Tis on you my hopes are set,
In manliness, in kindliness, in justice,
   To make Erin a nation yet;
Self-respecting, self-relying, self-advancing,
   In union or in severance, free and strong,
And if God grant this, then, under God, to Thomas Davis,
   Let the greater praise belong!

38   *Cashel of Munster*
          (*From the Irish*)

I'D wed you without herds, without money, or rich array,
And I'd wed you on a dewy morning at day-dawn grey;
My bitter woe it is, love, that we are not far away
In Cashel town, though the bare deal board were our mar-
   riage bed this day!

Oh, fair maid, remember the green hillside,
Remember how I hunted about the valleys wide;
Time now has worn me; my locks are turned to grey,
The year is scarce and I am poor, but send me not, love,
    away!

Oh, deem not my blood is of base strain, my girl,
Oh, deem not my birth was as the birth of the churl;
Marry me, and prove me, and say soon you will,
That noble blood is written on my right side still!

My purse holds no red gold, no coin of the silver white,
No herds are mine to drive through the long twilight!
But the pretty girl that would take me, all bare though I
    be and lone,
Oh, I'd take her with me kindly to the county Tyrone.

Oh, my girl, I can see 'tis in trouble you are,
And, oh, my girl, I see 'tis your people's reproach you bear:
'I am a girl in trouble for his sake with whom I fly,
And, oh, may no other maiden know such reproach as I!'

39   *The Coolun*

(*From the Irish*)

O HAD you seen the Coolun
    Walking down by the cuckoo's street,
With the dew of the meadow shining
    On her milk-white twinkling feet!
My love she is, and my coleen oge,[1]
    And she dwells in Bal'nagar;
And she bears the palm of beauty bright
    From the fairest that in Erin are.

[1] *cailín óg*: young girl.

SAMUEL FERGUSON

In Bal'nagar is the Coolun,
  Like the berry on the bough her cheek;
Bright beauty dwells for ever
  On her fair neck and ringlets sleek;
Oh, sweeter is her mouth's soft music
  Than the lark or thrush at dawn,
Or the blackbird in the greenwood singing
  Farewell to the setting sun.

Rise up, my boy! make ready
  My horse, for I forth would ride,
To follow the modest damsel,
  Where she walks on the green hillside:
For ever since our youth were we plighted
  In faith, troth, and wedlock true—
She is sweeter to me nine times over,
  Than organ or cuckoo!

For, ever since my Childhood
  I've loved the fair and darling child;
But our people came between us,
  And with lucre our pure love defiled:
Ah, my woe it is, and my bitter pain,
  And I weep it night and day,
That the coleen bawn[1] of my early love
  Is torn from my heart away.

Sweetheart and faithful treasure,
  Be constant still, and true;
Nor for want of herds and houses
  Leave one who would ne'er leave you.

[1] *cailín bán*: fair girl.

I'll pledge you the blessèd Bible,
  Without and eke within,
That the faithful God will provide for us,
  Without thanks to kith or kin.

Oh, love, do you remember
  When we lay all night alone,
Beneath the ash in the winter storm,
  When the oak wood round did groan?
No shelter then from the blast had we,
  The bitter blast or sleet,
But your gown to wrap about our heads,
  And my coat around our feet.

40　　　　　　　　*Dear Dark Head*

(*From the Irish*)

PUT your head, darling, darling, darling,
  Your darling black head my heart above;
Oh, mouth of honey, with the thyme for fragrance,
  Who, with heart in breast, could deny you love?

Oh, many and many a young girl for me is pining,
  Letting her locks of gold to the cold wind free,
For me, the foremost of our gay young fellows;
  But I'd leave a hundred, pure love, for thee!

Then put your head, darling, darling, darling,
  Your darling black head my heart above;
Oh, mouth of honey, with the thyme for fragrance,
  Who, with heart in breast, could deny you love?

41 *Páistín Fionn*[1]

(*From the Irish*)

OH, my fair Pastheen is my heart's delight,
Her gay heart laughs in her blue eye bright;
Like the apple-blossom her bosom white,
And her neck like the swan's on a March morn bright.

Chorus

Then, Oro, come with me! come with me! come with me!
Oro, come with me! brown girl, sweet!
And oh! I would go through snow and sleet,
If you would come with me, brown girl, sweet.

Love of my heart, my fair Pastheen!
Her cheeks are red as the rose's sheen,
But my lips have tasted no more, I ween,
Than the glass I drink to the health of my queen!

Were I in the town where's mirth and glee,
Or 'twixt two barrels of barley bree,
With my fair Pastheen upon my knee,
'Tis I would drink to her pleasantly!

Nine nights I lay in longing and pain,
Betwixt two bushes, beneath the rain,
Thinking to see you, love, again;
But whistle and call were all in vain!

I'll leave my people, both friend and foe;
From all the girls in the world I'll go;
But from you, sweetheart, oh, never, oh no!
Till I lie in the coffin stretched cold and low!

[1] *Páistín Fionn*: Fair little child.

THOMAS DAVIS
1814–1845

42 *Lament for the Death of
Eoghan Ruadh[1] O'Neill*

Time: 10 November 1649. Scene: Ormond's Camp, Co. Waterford.
Speakers: a Veteran of Eoghan O'Neill's clan, and one of the horsemen
just arrived with an account of his death.

'DID they dare, did they dare, to slay Eoghan Ruadh
    O'Neill?'
'Yes, they slew with poison him they feared to meet with
    steel.'
'May God wither up their hearts! May their blood cease to
    flow!
May they walk in living death, who poisoned Eoghan
    Ruadh!

'Though it break my heart to hear, say again the bitter
    words.'
'From Derry, against Cromwell, he marched to measure
    swords;
But the weapon of the Saxon met him on his way,
And he died at Cloch Uachtar, upon Saint Leonard's day.'

Wail, wail ye for the Mighty One! Wail, wail ye for the
    Dead;
Quench the hearth, and hold the breath—with ashes strew
    the head.
How tenderly we loved him! How deeply we deplore!
Holy Saviour! but to think we shall never see him more!

---

[1] *Eoghan Ruadh*: Red-haired Owen.

'Sagest in the council was he, kindest in the Hall:
Sure we never won a battle—'twas Eoghan won them all.
Had he lived—had he lived—our dear country had been free;
But he's dead, but he's dead, and 'tis slaves we'll ever be.

'O'Farrell and Clanricarde, Preston and Red Hugh,
Audley and MacMahon—ye are valiant, wise, and true;
But—what, what are ye all to our darling who is gone?
The Rudder of our ship was he, our Castle's corner-stone!

'Wail, wail him through the Island! Weep, weep for our
        pride!
Would that on the battle-field our gallant chief had died!
Weep the Victor of Benburb—weep him, young man and
        old;
Weep for him, ye women—your Beautiful lies cold!

'We thought you would not die—we were sure you would
        not go,
And leave us in our utmost need to Cromwell's cruel
        blow—
Sheep without a shepherd, when the snow shuts out the
        sky—
Oh! why did you leave us, Eoghan? Why did you die?

'Soft as woman's was your voice, O'Neill! bright was
        your eye,
Oh! why did you leave us, Eoghan? why did you die?
Your troubles are all over, you're at rest with God on high;
But we're slaves, and we're orphans, Eoghan!—why did
        you die?'

EMILY BRONTË

1818–1848

43   *Remembrance*

COLD in the earth—and the deep snow piled above thee,
Far, far removed, cold in the dreary grave!
Have I forgot, my only Love, to love thee,
Severed at last by Time's all-severing wave?

Now, when alone, do my thoughts no longer hover
Over the mountains, on that northern shore,
Resting their wings where heath and fern-leaves cover,
Thy noble heart for ever, ever more?

Cold in the earth—and fifteen wild Decembers
From those brown hills, have melted into spring:
Faithful, indeed, is the spirit that remembers
After such years of change and suffering!

Sweet Love of youth, forgive, if I forget thee,
While the World's tide is bearing me along;
Other desires and other hopes beset me,
Hopes which obscure, but cannot do thee wrong!

No later light has lightened up my heaven,
No second morn has ever shone for me;
All my life's bliss from thy dear life was given—
All my life's bliss is in the grave with thee.

But when the days of gold dreams had perished,
And even Despair was powerless to destroy,
Then did I learn how existence could be cherished,
Strengthened, and fed, without the aid of joy.

Then did I check the tears of useless passion,
Weaned my young soul from yearning after thine;
Sternly denied its burning wish to hasten
Down to that tomb already more than mine!

And, even yet, I dare not let it languish,
Dare not indulge in Memory's rapturous pain;
Once drinking deep of that divinest anguish,
How could I seek the empty world again?

44   *Warning and Reply*

In the earth, the earth, thou shalt be laid
A grey stone standing over thee;
Black mould beneath thee spread
And black mould to cover thee.

'Well, there is rest there,
So fast come thy prophecy;
The time when my sunny hair
Shall with grass roots twinèd be.'

But cold, cold is that resting place,
Shut out from Joy and Liberty,
And all who loved thy living face
Will shrink from its gloom and thee.

'Not so: *here* the world is chill,
And sworn friends fall from me;
But *there*, they'll own me still
And prize my memory.'

Farewell, then, all that love,
All that deep sympathy:
Sleep on; Heaven laughs above,
Earth never misses thee.

Turf-sod and tombstone drear
Part human company;
One heart broke only there—
That heart was worthy thee!

45   *No Coward Soul*

No coward soul is mine,
No trembler in the world's storm-troubled sphere:
I see Heaven's glories shine,
And Faith shines equal, arming me from Fear.

O God within my breast,
Almighty, ever-praising Deity!
Life, that in me has rest
As I, undying Life have power in thee!

Vain are the thousand creeds
That move men's hearts, unutterably vain;
Worthless as withered weeds,
Or idlest froth amid the boundless main,

To waken doubt in one,
Holding so fast by thy infinity,
So surely anchored on
The steadfast rock of Immortality.

With wide-embracing love
Thy Spirit animates eternal years,
Pervades and broods above,
Changes, sustains, dissolves, creates and rears.

Though Earth and moon were gone,
And suns and universes ceased to be,
And Thou wert left alone,
Every Existence would exist in Thee.

There is not room for Death,
Nor atom that His might could render void:
Since Thou art Being and Breath,
And what Thou art may never be destroyed.

46   *The Old Stoic*

RICHES I hold in light esteem
And Love I laugh to scorn
And lust of Fame was but a dream
That vanished with the morn—

And if I pray, the only prayer
That moves my lips for me
Is—'Leave the heart that now I bear
And give me liberty.'

Yes, as my swift days near their goal
'Tis all that I implore—
In life and death a chainless soul
With courage to endure!

47   *A Little While, A Little While*

A LITTLE while, a little while,
The noisy crowd are barred away;
And I can sing and I can smile
A little while I've holyday!

Where wilt thou go, my harassed heart?
Full many a land invites thee now;
And places near and far apart
Have rest for thee, my weary brow.

There is a spot 'mid barren hills
Where winter howls and driving rain,
But if the dreary tempest chills
There is a light that warms again.

The house is old, the trees are bare
And moonless bends the misty dome
But what on earth is half so dear,
So longed for as the hearth of home?

The mute bird sitting on the stone,
The dank moss dripping from the wall,
The garden-walk with weeds o'ergrown,
I love them—how I love them all!

Shall I go there? or shall I seek
Another clime, another sky,
Where tongues familiar music speak
In accents dear to memory?

Yes, as I mused, the naked room,
The flickering firelight died away
And from the midst of cheerless gloom
I passed to bright, unclouded day—

A little and a lone green lane
That opened on a common wide;
A distant, dreamy, dim blue chain
Of mountains circling every side;

A heaven so clear, an earth so calm,
So sweet, so soft, so hushed an air
And, deepening still the dream-like charm,
Wild moor-sheep feeding everywhere—

That was the scene; I knew it well,
I knew the path-ways far and near
That winding o'er each billowy swell
Marked out the tracks of wandering deer.

Could I have lingered but an hour
It well had paid a week of toil,
But truth has banished fancy's power;
I hear my dungeon bars recoil—

Even as I stood with raptured eye
Absorbed in bliss so deep and dear
My hour of rest had fleeted by
And given me back to weary care.

FRANCES ALEXANDER

1820–1895

48 *His are the Thousand Sparkling Rills*

His are the thousand sparkling rills
    That from a thousand fountains burst,
And fill with music all the hills;
    And yet He saith, 'I thirst.'

All fiery pangs on battle-fields,
    On fever beds where sick men toss,
Are in that human cry He yields
    To anguish on the cross.

But more than pains that racked Him then
  Was the deep longing thirst Divine
That thirsted for the souls of men:
  Dear Lord! and one was mine.

O Love most patient, give me grace;
  Make all my soul athirst for Thee;
That parched dry Lip, that fading Face,
  That Thirst were all for me.

49   *The Breastplate of St. Patrick*
                (*From the Irish*)

I BIND unto myself to-day
  The strong Name of the Trinity,
By invocation of the same,
  The Three in One and One in Three.

I bind this day to me for ever,
  By pow'r of faith, Christ's incarnation;
His baptism in Jordan river;
  His death on Cross for my salvation;
His bursting from the spicèd tomb;
  His riding up the heavenly way;
His coming at the day of doom;
  I bind unto myself to-day.

I bind unto myself the power
  Of the great love of Cherubim;
The sweet 'Well done' in judgment hour,
  The service of the Seraphim,
Confessors' faith, Apostles' word,
  The patriarchs' prayers, the Prophets' scrolls,
All good deeds done unto the Lord,
  And purity of virgin souls.

I bind unto myself to-day
  The virtues of the star-lit heaven,
The glorious sun's life-giving ray,
  The whiteness of the moon at even,
The flashing of the lightning free,
  The whirling wind's tempestuous shocks,
The stable earth, the deep salt sea
  Around the old eternal rocks.

I bind unto myself to-day
  The pow'r of God to hold, and lead,
His eye to watch, His might to stay,
  His ear to hearken to my need;
The wisdom of my God to teach,
  His hand to guide, His shield to ward;
The Word of God to give me speech,
  His heavenly host to be my guard:

Against the demon snares of sin,
  The vice that gives temptation force,
The natural lusts that war within,
  The hostile men that mar my course;
Or few or many, far or nigh,
  In every place, and in all hours,
Against their fierce hostility,
  I bind to me these holy powers:

Against all Satan's spells and wiles,
  Against false words of heresy,
Against the knowledge that defiles,
  Against the heart's idolatry,
Against the wizard's evil craft,
  Against the death-wound and the burning,
The choking wave, the poisoned shaft,
  Protect me, Christ, till Thy returning.

Christ be with me, Christ within me,
　Christ behind me, Christ before me,
Christ beside me, Christ to win me,
　Christ to comfort and restore me,
Christ beneath me, Christ above me,
　Christ in quiet, Christ in danger,
Christ in hearts of all that love me,
　Christ in mouth of friend and stranger.

I bind unto myself the Name,
　The strong Name of the Trinity;
By invocation of the same,
　The Three in One, and One in Three.
Of Whom all nature hath creation;
　Eternal Father, Spirit, Word:
Praise to the Lord of my salvation,
　Salvation is of Christ the Lord.

JOHN KELLS INGRAM
1823–1907

50　　*The Memory of the Dead*

WHO fears to speak of Ninety-eight?
Who blushes at the name?
When cowards mock the patriot's fate,
Who hangs his head for shame?
He's all a knave, or half a slave,
Who slights his country thus;
But a true man, like you, man,
Will fill your glass with us.

We drink the memory of the brave,
The faithful and the few;
Some lie far off beyond the wave,
Some sleep in Ireland, too;
All, all are gone; but still lives on
The fame of those who died;
All true men, like you, men,
Remember them with pride.

Some on the shores of distant lands
Their weary hearts have laid,
And by the stranger's heedless hands
Their lonely graves were made;
But though their clay be far away
Beyond the Atlantic foam,
In true men, like you, men,
Their spirit's still at home.

The dust of some is Irish earth,
Among their own they rest,
And the same land that gave them birth
Has caught them to her breast;
And we will pray that from their clay
Full many a race may start
Of true men, like you, men,
To act as brave a part.

They rose in dark and evil days
To right their native land;
They kindled here a living blaze
That nothing shall withstand.
Alas! that might can vanquish right—
They fell and passed away;
But true men, like you, men,
Are plenty here to-day.

Then here's their memory—may it be
For us a guiding light,
To cheer our strife for liberty,
And teach us to unite—
Through good and ill, be Ireland's still,
Though sad as theirs your fate,
And true men be you, men,
Like those of Ninety-eight.

WILLIAM ALLINGHAM

1824–1889

51   *The Fairies*

(*A Child's Song*)

Up the airy mountain,
    Down the rushy glen,
We daren't go a-hunting
    For fear of little men;
Wee folk, good folk,
    Trooping all together;
Green jacket, red cap,
    And white owl's feather!

Down along the rocky shore
    Some make their home—
They live on crispy pancakes
    Of yellow tide-foam;
Some in the reeds
    Of the black mountain lake,
With frogs for their watch-dogs,
    All night awake.

High on the hill-top
    The old King sits;
He is now so old and grey
    He's nigh lost his wits.
With a bridge of white mist
    Columbkill he crosses,
On his stately journeys
    From Slieveleague to Rosses;
Or going up with music
    On cold starry nights,
To sup with the Queen
    Of the gay Northern Lights.

They stole little Bridget
    For seven years long;
When she came down again
    Her friends were all gone.
They took her lightly back,
   Between the night and morrow;
They thought that she was fast asleep,
    But she was dead with sorrow.
They have kept her ever since
    Deep within the lake,
On a bed of flag-leaves,
    Watching till she wake.

By the craggy hill-side,
    Through the mosses bare,
They have planted thorn-trees
    For pleasure here and there.
Is any man so daring
    As dig one up in spite,
He shall find their sharpest thorns
    In his bed at night.

Up the airy mountain,
      Down the rushy glen,
We daren't go a-hunting
      For fear of little men;
Wee folk, good folk,
      Trooping all together;
Green jacket, red cap,
      And white owl's feather!

52   *Abbey Asaroe*

GREY, grey is Abbey Asaroe, by Belashanny town,
It has neither doors nor windows, the walls are broken down;
The carven-stones lie scattered in briar and nettle-bed;
The only feet are those that come at burial of the dead.
A little rocky rivulet runs murmuring to the tide,
Singing a song of ancient days, in sorrow, not in pride;
The boortree and the lightsome ash across the portal grow,
And heaven itself is now the roof of Abbey Asaroe.

It looks beyond the harbour-stream to Gulban mountain blue;
It hears the voice of Erna's fall,—Atlantic breakers too;
High ships go sailing past it; the sturdy clank of oars
Brings in the salmon-boat to haul a net upon the shores;
And this way to his home-creek, when the summer day is done,
Slow sculls the weary fisherman across the setting sun;
While green with corn is Sheegus Hill, his cottage white below;
But grey at every season is Abbey Asaroe.

There stood one day a poor old man above its broken
    bridge;
He heard no running rivulet, he saw no mountain-ridge;
He turned his back on Sheegus Hill and viewed with misty
    sight
The Abbey walls, the burial-ground with crosses ghostly
    white;
Under a weary weight of years he bowed upon his staff,
Perusing in the present time the former's epitaph;
For, grey and wasted like the walls, a figure full of woe,
This man was of the blood of them who founded Asaroe.

From Derry to Bundrowas Tower, Tirconnell broad was
    theirs;
Spearmen and plunder, bards and wine, and holy abbot's
    prayers;
With chanting always in the house that they had builded high
To God and to Saint Bernard,—where at last they came to
    die.
At worst, no workhouse grave for him! the ruins of his race
Shall rest among the ruin'd stones of this their saintly place.
The fond old man was weeping; and tremulous and slow
Along the rough and crooked lane he crept from Asaroe.

53   *Four Ducks on a Pond*

       FOUR ducks on a pond,
       A grass-bank beyond,
       A blue sky of spring,
       White birds on the wing:
       What a little thing
       To remember for years—
       To remember with tears!

54   *Adieu to Belashanny*[1]

ADIEU to Belashanny! where I was bred and born;
Go where I may, I'll think of you as sure as night and morn:
The kindly spot, the friendly town, where every one is
        known,
And not a face in all the place but partly seems my own;
There's not a house or window, there's not a field or hill,
But, east or west, in foreign lands, I'll recollect them still.
I leave my warm heart with you, tho' my back I'm forced
        to turn—
Adieu to Belashanny, and the winding banks of Erne!

No more on pleasant evenings we'll saunter down the Mall,
When the trout is rising to the fly, the salmon to the fall.
The boat comes straining on her net, and heavily she creeps,
Cast off, cast off—she feels the oars, and to her berth she
        sweeps;
Now fore and aft keep hauling, and gathering up the clew,
Till a silver wave of salmon rolls in among the crew.
Then they may sit, with pipes a-lit, and many a joke and
        'yarn';—
Adieu to Belashanny, and the winding banks of Erne!

The music of the waterfall, the mirror of the tide,
When all the green-hill'd harbour is full from side to side.
From Portnasun to Bulliebawns, and round the Abbey
        Bay,
From rocky Inis Saimer to Coolnargit sand-hills grey;
While far upon the southern line, to guard it like a wall,
The Leitrim mountains clothed in blue gaze calmly over
        all,

    [1] Ballyshannon, at the mouth of the Erne, Co. Donegal.

And watch the ship sail up or down, the red flag at her
    stern;—
Adieu to these, adieu to all the winding banks of Erne!

Farewell to you, Kildoney lads, and them that pull an oar,
A lug-sail set, or haul a net from the Point to Mullagh-
    more;
From Killybegs to bold Slieveleague, that ocean-moun-
    tain steep,
Six hundred yards in air aloft, six hundred in the deep;
From Dooran to the Fairy Bridge, and round by Tullen
    Strand,
Level and long, and white with waves, where gull and cur-
    lew stand;
Head out to sea, when on your lea the breakers you
    discern!—
Adieu to all that billowy coast, and winding banks of Erne!

Farewell, Coolmore, Bundoran! and your summer crowds
    that run
From inland homes to see with joy th' Atlantic-setting sun;
To breathe the buoyant salted air, and sport among the
    waves;
To gather shells on sandy beach, and tempt the gloomy
    caves;
To watch the flowing, ebbing tide, the boats, the crabs, the
    fish;
Young men and maids to meet and smile, and form a tender
    wish;
The sick and old in search of health, for all things have their
    turn—
And I must quit my native shore, and the winding banks of
    Erne!

Farewell to every white cascade from the Harbour to
　　Belleek,
And every pool where fins may rest, and ivy-shaded creek;
The sloping fields, the lofty rocks, where ash and holly
　　grow,
The one split yew-tree gazing on the curving flood below;
The Lough, that winds through islands under Turaw
　　mountain green;
And Castle Caldwell's stretching woods, with tranquil bays
　　between;
And Breesie Hill, and many a pond among the heath and
　　fern,—
For I must say adieu—adieu to the winding banks of Erne!

The thrush will call through Camlin groves the live-long
　　summer day;
The waters run by mossy cliffs, and banks with wild flowers
　　gay;
The girls will bring their work and sing beneath a twisted
　　thorn,
Or stray with sweethearts down the path among the grow-
　　ing corn;
Along the river-side they go, where I have often been,
O, never shall I see again the days that I have seen!
A thousand chances are to one I never may return,—
Adieu to Belashanny, and the winding banks of Erne.

Adieu to evening dances, when merry neighbours meet,
And the fiddle says to boys and girls, 'Get up and shake
　　your feet!'
To 'shanchus'[1] and wise old talk of Erin's days gone by—
Who trench'd the rath on such a hill, and where the bones
　　may lie

---

[1] *seanchas*: the telling of stories.

Of saint, or king, or warrior chief; with tales of fairy
    power,
And tender ditties sweetly sung to pass the twilight hour.
The mournful song of exile is now for me to learn—
Adieu, my dear companions on the winding banks or
    Erne!

Now measure from the Commons down to each end of the
    Port,
Beyond the Abbey, Moy and Knather,—I wish no one any
    hurt;
The Main Street, Back Street, College Lane, the Mall and
    Portnasun,
If any foes of mine are there, I pardon every one.
I hope that man and womankind will do the same by me;
For my heart is sore and heavy at voyaging the sea.
My loving friends I'll bear in mind, and often fondly turn
To think of Belashanny and the winding banks of Erne!

If ever I'm a money'd man, I mean, please God, to cast
My golden anchor in the place where youthful years were
    pass'd;
Though heads that now are black and brown must mean-
    while gather grey,
New faces rise by every hearth, and old ones drop away—
Yet dearer still that Irish hill than all the world beside;
It's home, sweet home, where'er I roam, through lands
    and waters wide.
And if the Lord allows me, I surely will return
To my native Belashanny and the winding banks of Erne.

55 *A Dream*

I HEARD the dogs howl in the moonlight night;
I went to the window to see the sight;
All the Dead that ever I knew
Going one by one and two by two.

On they pass'd, and on they pass'd;
Townsfellows all, from first to last;
Born in the moonlight of the lane,
Quench'd in the heavy shadow again.

Schoolmates, marching as when we play'd
At soldiers once—but now more staid;
Those were the strangest sight to me
Who were drown'd, I knew, in the awful sea.

Straight and handsome folk; bent and weak too;
Some that I loved, and gasp'd to speak to;
Some but a day in their churchyard bed;
Some that I had not known were dead.

A long, long crowd—where each seem'd lonely,
Yet of them all there was one, one only,
Raised a head or look'd my way;
She linger'd a moment,—she might not stay.

How long since I saw that fair pale face!
Ah! Mother dear! might I only place
My head on thy breast, a moment to rest,
While thy hand on my tearful cheek were prest.

On, on a moving bridge they made
Across the moon-stream from shade to shade,
Young and old, women and men;
Many long forgot, but remember'd then.

And first there came a bitter laughter;
A sound of tears the moment after;
And then a music so lofty and gay,
That every morning, day by day,
I strive to recall it if I may.

THOMAS D'ARCY McGEE

1825–1868

56   *The Celts*

LONG, long ago, beyond the misty space
        Of twice a thousand years,
In Erin old there dwelt a mighty race,
        Taller than Roman spears;
Like oaks and towers they had a giant grace,
        Were fleet as deers,
With wind and waves they made their 'biding place,
        These western shepherd seers.

Their Ocean-God was Manannan MacLir,
        Whose angry lips,
In their white foam, full often would inter
        Whole fleets of ships;
Cromah their Day-God, and their Thunderer
        Made morning and eclipse;
Bride was their Queen of Song, and unto her
        They prayed with fire-touched lips.

Great were their deeds, their passions and their sports;
    With clay and stone
They piled on strath and shore those mystic forts,
    Not yet o'erthrown;
On cairn-crowned hills they held their council-courts;
    While youths alone,
With giant dogs, explored the elk resorts,
    And brought them down.

Of these was Finn, the father of the Bard,
    Whose ancient song
Over the clamour of all change is heard,
    Sweet-voiced and strong.
Finn once o'ertook Grania, the golden-haired,
    The fleet and young;
From her the lovely, and from him the feared,
    The primal poet sprung.

Ossian! two thousand years of mist and change
    Surround thy name—
Thy Fenian heroes now no longer range
    The hills of fame.
The very names of Finn and Gaul sound strange—
    Yet thine the same—
By miscalled lake and desecrated grange—
    Remains, and shall remain!

The Druid's altar and the Druid's creed
    We scarce can trace,
There is not left an undisputed deed
    Of all your race,
Save your majestic song, which hath their speed,
    And strength and grace;
In that sole song, they live and love, and bleed—
    It bears them on through space.

O, inspired giant! shall we e'er behold,
    In our own time,
One fit to speak your spirit on the wold,
    Or seize your rhyme?
One pupil of the past, as mighty-souled
    As in the prime,
Were the fond, fair, and beautiful, and bold—
    They of your song sublime!

GEORGE SIGERSON

1836–1925

57   *Love's Despair*

(*From the Irish*)

I AM desolate,
    Bereft by bitter fate;
No cure beneath the skies can save me,
    No cure on sea or strand,
    Nor in any human hand—
But hers, this paining wound who gave me.

I know not night from day,
    Nor thrust from cuckoo grey,
Nor cloud from the sun that shines above thee—
    Nor freezing cold from heat,
    Nor friend—if friend I meet—
I but know—heart's love!—I love thee.

Love that my Life began,
   Love, that will close life's span,
Love that grows ever by love-giving:
   Love, from the first to last,
   Love, till all life be passed,
Love that loves on after living!

   This love I gave to thee,
   For pain love has given me,
Love that can fail or falter never—
   But, spite of earth above,
   Guards thee, my Flower of love,
Thou marvel-maid of life for ever.

   Bear all things evidence,
   Thou art my very sense,
My past, my present, and my morrow!
   All else on earth is crossed,
   All in the world is lost—
Lost all—but the great love-gift of sorrow.

   My life not life, but death;
   My voice not voice—a breath;
No sleep, no quiet—thinking ever
   On thy fair phantom face,
   Queen eyes and royal grace,
Lost loveliness that leaves me never.

   I pray thee grant but this—
   From thy dear mouth one kiss,
That the pang of death-despair pass over:
   Or bid make ready nigh
   The place where I shall lie,
For aye, thy leal and silent lover.

JOHN TODHUNTER

1839–1916

Aghadoe

THERE'S a glen in Aghadoe, Aghadoe, Aghadoe,
There's a green and silent glade in Aghadoe,
    Where we met, my Love and I, Love's fair planet in the
      sky,
O'er that sweet and silent glen in Aghadoe.

There's a glen in Aghadoe, Aghadoe, Aghadoe,
There's a deep and secret glen in Aghadoe.
    Where I hid him from the eyes of the redcoats and their
      spies
That year the trouble came to Aghadoe!

Oh! my curse on one black heart in Aghadoe, Aghadoe,
On Shaun Dhuv,[1] my mother's son in Aghadoe,
    When your throat fries in hell's drouth salt the flame be
      in your mouth,
For the treachery you did in Aghadoe!

For they tracked me to that glen in Aghadoe, Aghadoe,
When the price was on his head in Aghadoe;
    O'er the mountain through the wood, as I stole to him
      with food,
When in hiding low he lay in Aghadoe.

But they never took him living in Aghadoe, Aghadoe;
With the bullets in his heart in Aghadoe,
    There he lay, the head—my breast keeps the warmth
      where once 'twould rest—
Gone, to win the traitor's gold from Aghadoe!

[1] Seán Dubh: Black-haired John.

I walked to Mallow Town from Aghadoe, Aghadoe,
Brought his head from the gaol's gate to Aghadoe,
   Then I covered him with fern, and I piled on him the
     cairn,
Like an Irish king he sleeps in Aghadoe.

EDWARD DOWDEN

1843–1913

59   *In the Cathedral Close*

IN the Dean's porch a nest of clay
   With five small tenants may be seen,
Five solemn faces, each as wise
   As though its owner were a Dean;

Five downy fledglings in a row,
   Packed close, as in the antique pew
The school-girls are, whose foreheads clear
   At the *Venite* shine on you.

Day after day the swallows sit
   With scarce a stir, with scarce a sound,
But dreaming and digesting much
   They grow thus wise and soft and round.

They watch the Canons come to dine,
   And hear the mullion-bars across,
Over the fragrant fruit and wine
   Deep talk of rood-screen and reredos.

Her hands with field-flowers drench'd, a child
  Leaps past in wind-blown dress and hair,
The swallows turn their heads askew—
  Five judges deem that she is fair.

Prelusive touches sound within,
  Straightway they recognise the sign,
And, blandly nodding, they approve
  The minuet of Rubenstein.

They mark the cousins' schoolboy talk,
  (Male birds flown wide from minster bell),
And blink at each broad term of art,
  Binomial or bicycle.

Ah! downy young ones, soft and warm,
  Doth such a stillness mask from sight
Such swiftness? Can such peace conceal
  Passion and ecstasy of flight?

Yet somewhere 'mid yon Eastern suns,
  Under a white Greek architrave
At morn, or when the shaft of fire
  Lies large upon the Indian wave,

A sense of something dear gone-by
  Will stir, strange longings thrill the heart
For a small world embowered and close,
  Of which ye some time were a part.

The dew-drenched flowers, the child's glad eyes
  Your joy inhuman shall control,
And in your wings a light and wind
  Shall move from the Maestro's soul.

60   *Oasis*

LET them go by—the heats, the doubts, the strife;
  I can sit here and care not for them now,
Dreaming beside the glimmering wave of life
  Once more,—I know not how.

There is a murmur in my heart, I hear
  Faint, O so faint, some air I used to sing;
It stirs my sense; and odours dim and dear
  The meadow-breezes bring.

Just this way did the quiet twilights fade
  Over the fields and happy homes of men,
While one bird sang as now, piercing the shade,
  Long since,—I know not when.

ARTHUR O'SHAUGHNESSY

1844–1881

61   From *Ode*

WE are the music-makers,
  And we are the dreamers of dreams,
Wandering by lone sea-breakers,
  And sitting by desolate streams;—
World-losers and world-forsakers,
  On whom the pale moon gleams:
Yet we are the movers and shakers
  Of the world for ever, it seems.

We, in the ages lying
   In the buried past of the earth,
Built Nineveh with our sighing,
   And Babel itself with our mirth;
And o'erthrew them with prophesying
   To the old of the new world's worth;
For each age is a dream that is dying,
   Or one that is coming to birth.

62
The Appointment

'Tis late; the astronomer in his lonely height,
Exploring all the dark, descries afar
Orbs that like distant isles of splendour are,
And mornings whitening in the infinite.

Like winnowed grain the worlds go by in flight,
Or swarm in glistening spaces nebular;
He summons one dishevelled wandering star,—
Return ten centuries hence on such a night.

The star will come. It dare not by one hour
Cheat Science, or falsify her calculation;
Men will have passed, but watchful in the tower

Man shall remain in sleepless contemplation;
And should all men have perished there in turn,
Truth in their place would watch that star's return.
          (*From the French of Sully Prudhomme*)

HON. EMILY LAWLESS
1845–1913

63

After Aughrim

SHE said, 'They gave me of their best,
They lived, they gave their lives for me;
I tossed them to the howling waste,
And flung them to the foaming sea.'

She said, 'I never gave them aught,
Not mine the power, if mine the will;
I let them starve, I let them bleed,—
They bled and starved, and loved me still.'

She said, 'Ten times they fought for me,
Ten times they strove with might and main,
Ten times I saw them beaten down,
Ten times they rose, and fought again.'

She said, 'I stayed alone at home,
A dreary woman, grey and cold;
I never asked them how they fared,
Yet still they loved me as of old.'

She said, 'I never called them sons,
I almost ceased to breathe their name,
Then caught it echoing down the wind,
Blown backwards from the lips of Fame.'

She said, 'Not mine, not mine that fame;
Far over sea, far over land,
Cast forth like rubbish from my shores,
They won it yonder, sword in hand.'

She said, 'God knows they owe me naught,
I tossed them to the foaming sea,
I tossed them to the howling waste,
Yet still their love comes home to me.'

64   *Clare Coast*

Circa 1720

SEE, cold island, we stand
Here to-night on your shore,
To-night, but never again;
Lingering a moment more.
See, beneath us our boat
Tugs at its tightening chain,
Holds out its sail to the breeze,
Pants to be gone again.
Off then with shouts and mirth,
Off with laughter and jests,
Mirth and song on our lips,
Hearts like lead in our breasts.

Death and the grave behind,
Death, and a traitor's bier;
Honour and fame before,
Why do we linger here?
Why do we stand and gaze,
Fools, whom fools despise,
Fools untaught by the years,
Fools renounced by the wise?
Heartsick, a moment more,
Heartsick, sorry, fierce,
Lingering, lingering on,
Dreaming the dreams of yore;

Dreaming the dreams of our youth,
Dreaming the days when we stood
Joyous, expectant, serene,
Glad, exultant of mood,
Singing with hearts afire,
Singing with joyous strain,
Singing aloud in our pride,
'We shall redeem her again!'
Ah, not to-night that strain,—
Silent to-night we stand,
A scanty, a toil-worn crew,
Strangers, foes in the land!
Gone the light of our youth,
Gone for ever, and gone
Hope with the beautiful eyes,
Who laughed as she lured us on;
Lured us to danger and death,
To honour, perchance to fame—
Empty fame at the best,
Glory half dimmed with shame.
War-battered dogs are we
Fighters in every clime,
Fillers of trench and grave,
Mockers, bemocked by time.
War-dogs, hungry and grey,
Gnawing a naked bone,
Fighters in every clime,
Every cause but our own.

See us, cold isle of our love!
Coldest, saddest of isles—
Cold as the hopes of our youth,
Cold as your own wan smiles.

Coldly your streams outpour,
Each apart on the height,
Trickling, indifferent, slow,
Lost in the hush of the night.
Colder, sadder the clouds,
Comfortless bringers of rain;
Desolate daughters of air,
Sweep o'er your sad grey plain
Hiding the form of your hills,
Hiding your low sand dunes;
But coldest, saddest, oh isle!
Are the homeless hearts of your sons.

Coldest, and saddest there,
In yon sun-lit land of the south,
Where we sicken and sorrow and pine,
And the jest flies from mouth to mouth,
And the church bells crash overhead,
And the idle hours flit by,
And the beaded wine-cups clink,
And the sun burns fierce in the sky;
And your exiles, the merry of heart,
Laugh and boast with the best,—
Boast, and extol their part,
Boast, till some lifted brow,
Crossed with a line severe,
Seems with displeasure to ask,
'Are these loud braggarts we hear,
Are they the sons of the West,
The wept-for, the theme of songs,
The exiled, the injured, the banned,
The men of a thousand wrongs?'

Fool, did you never hear
Of sunshine which broke through rain?
Sunshine which came with storm?
Laughter that rang of pain?
Boastings begotten of grief,
Vauntings to hide a smart,
Braggings with trembling lip,
Tricks of a broken heart?

Sudden some wayward gleam,
Sudden some passing sound,—
The careless splash of an oar,
The idle bark of a hound,
A shadow crossing the sun,
An unknown step in the hall,
A nothing, a folly, a straw!—
Back it returns—all—all!
Back with the rush of a storm,
Back the old anguish and ill,
The sad, green landscape of home,
The small grey house by the hill,
The wide grey shores of the lake,
The low sky, seeming to weave
Its tender pitiful arms
Round the sick lone landscape at eve.
Back with its pains and its wrongs,
Back with its toils and its strife,
Back with its struggles and woe,
Back flows the stream of our life.
Darkened with treason and wrong,
Darkened with anguish and ruth,
Bitter, tumultuous, fierce,
Yet glad in the light of our youth.

So, cold island, we stand
Here to-night on your shore,—
To-night, but never again,
Lingering a moment more.
See, beneath us our boat
Tugs at its tightening chain,
Holds out its sail to the breeze,
Pants to be gone again.
Off then with shouts and mirth,
Off with laughter and jests,
Jests and song on our lips,
Hearts like lead in our breasts.

WILLIAM LARMINIE

1850–1900

65   *The Nameless Doon*[1]

WHO were the builders? Question not the silence
That settles on the lake for evermore,
Save when the sea-bird screams and to the islands
The echo answers from the steep-cliffed shore.
O half-remaining ruin, in the lore
Of human life a gap shall all deplore
Beholding thee; since thou art like the dead
Found slain, no token to reveal the why,
The name, the story. Some one murder'd
We know, we guess; and gazing upon thee,
And, filled by thy long silence of reply,
We guess some garnered sheaf of tragedy;—
Of tribe or nation slain so utterly

[1] *Dún*: a fort.

That even their ghosts are dead, and on their grave
Springeth no bloom of legend in its wildness;
And age by age weak washing round the islands
No faintest sigh of story lisps the wave.

AUGUSTA GREGORY

1852–1932

66   *Donal Oge*[1]*: Grief of a Girl's Heart*
(*From the Irish*)

O DONAL OGE, if you go across the sea,
Bring myself with you and do not forget it;
And you will have a sweetheart for fair days and market
    days,
And the daughter of the King of Greece beside you at night.

It is late last night the dog was speaking of you;
The snipe was speaking of you in her deep marsh.
It is you are the lonely bird through the woods;
And that you may be without a mate until you find me.

You promised me, and you said a lie to me,
That you would be before me where the sheep are flocked;
I gave a whistle and three hundred cries to you,
And I found nothing there but a bleating lamb.

You promised me a thing that was hard for you,
A ship of gold under a silver mast;
Twelve towns with a market in all of them,
And a fine white court by the side of the sea.

[1] *Donal Óg*: Young Donal.

You promised me a thing that is not possible,
That you would give me gloves of the skin of a fish;
That you would give me shoes of the skin of a bird;
And a suit of the dearest silk in Ireland.

O Donal Oge, it is I would be better to you
Than a high, proud, spendthrift lady:
I would milk the cow; I would bring help to you;
And if you were hard pressed, I would strike a blow for you.

O, ochone, and it's not with hunger
Or with wanting food, or drink, or sleep,
That I am growing thin, and my life is shortened;
But it is the love of a young man has withered me away.

It is early in the morning that I saw him coming,
Going along the road on the back of a horse;
He did not come to me; he made nothing of me;
And it is on my way home that I cried my fill.

When I go by myself to the Well of Loneliness,
I sit down and I go through my trouble;
When I see the world and do not see my boy,
He that has an amber shade in his hair.

It was on that Sunday I gave my love to you;
The Sunday that is last before Easter Sunday.
And myself on my knees reading the Passion;
And my two eyes giving love to you for ever.

O, aya! my mother, give myself to him;
And give him all that you have in the world;
Get out yourself to ask for alms,
And do not come back and forward looking for me.

My mother said to me not to be talking with you, to-day,
Or to-morrow, or on Sunday;
It was a bad time she took for telling me that;
It was shutting the door after the house was robbed.

My heart is as black as the blackness of the sloe,
Or as the black coal that is on the smith's forge;
Or as the sole of a shoe left in white halls;
It was you put that darkness over my life.

You have taken the east from me; you have taken the west
 from me,
You have taken what is before me and what is behind me;
You have taken the moon, you have taken the sun from me,
And my fear is great that you have taken God from me!

FANNY PARNELL

1854–1882

67   *After Death*

SHALL mine eyes behold thy glory, O my country?
 Shall mine eyes behold thy glory?
Or shall the darkness close around them, ere the sunblaze
 Break at last upon thy story?

When the nations ope for thee their queenly circle,
 As a sweet new sister hail thee,
Shall these lips be sealed in callous death and silence,
 That have known but to bewail thee?

Shall the ear be deaf that only loved thy praises,
 When all men their tribute bring thee?
Shall the mouth be clay that sang thee in thy squalor,
 When all poets' mouths shall sing thee?

Ah! the harpings and the salvos and the shoutings
   Of thy exiled sons returning!
I should hear, tho' dead and mouldered, and the grave-
    damps
   Should not chill my bosom's burning.

Ah! the tramp of feet victorious! I should hear them
   'Mid the shamrocks and the mosses,
And my heart should toss within the shroud and quiver,
   As a captive dreamer tosses.

I should turn and rend the cere-clothes round me,
   Giant sinews I should borrow—
Crying, 'O, my brothers, I have also loved her
   In her loneliness and sorrow!

'Let me join with you the jubilant procession;
   Let me chant with you her story;
Then contented I shall go back to the shamrocks,
   Now mine eyes have seen her glory!'

OSCAR WILDE

1854–1900

68   *Requiescat*

TREAD lightly, she is near
   Under the snow,
Speak gently, she can hear
   The daisies grow.

All her bright golden hair
   Tarnished with rust,
She that was young and fair
   Fallen to dust.

Lily-like, white as snow,
  She hardly knew
She was a woman, so
  Sweetly she grew.

Coffin-board, heavy stone
  Lie on her breast,
I vex my heart alone,
  She is at rest.

Peace, Peace, she cannot hear
  Lyre or sonnet,
All my life's buried here,
  Heap earth upon it.

69   *Theocritus*

            A Villanelle

O SINGER of Persephone!
  In the dim meadows desolate
Dost thou remember Sicily?

Still through the ivy flits the bee
  Where Amaryllis lies in state;
O singer of Persephone!

Simætha calls on Hecate
  And hears the wild dogs at the gate;
Dost thou remember Sicily?

Still by the light and laughing sea
  Poor Polypheme bemoans his fate:
O singer of Persephone!

And still in boyish rivalry
　　Young Daphnis challenges his mate:
Dost thou remember Sicily?

Slim Lacon keeps a goat for thee,
　　For thou the jocund shepherds wait,
O singer of Persephone!
Dost thou remember Sicily?

70　　From *The Ballad of Reading Gaol*

THERE is no chapel on the day
　　On which they hang a man:
The Chaplain's heart is far too sick,
　　Or his face is far too wan,
Or there is that written in his eyes
　　Which none should look upon.

So they kept us close till nigh on noon,
　　And then they rang the bell,
And the Warders with their jangling keys.
　　Opened each listening cell,
And down the iron stair we tramped,
　　Each from his separate Hell.

Out into God's sweet air we went,
　　But not in wonted way,
For this man's face was white with fear,
　　And that man's face was grey,
And I never saw sad men who looked
　　So wistfully at the day.

I never saw sad men who looked
  With such a wistful eye
Upon that little tent of blue
  We prisoners call the sky,
And at every careless cloud that passed
  In happy freedom by.

The Warders strutted up and down,
  And kept their herd of brutes,
Their uniforms were spic and span,
  And they wore their Sunday suits,
But we knew the work they had been at,
  By the quicklime on their boots.

For where a grave had opened wide,
  There was no grave at all:
Only a stretch of mud and sand
  By the hideous prison-wall,
And a little heap of burning lime,
  That the man should have his pall,

For he has a pall, this wretched man,
  Such as few men can claim:
Deep down below a prison-yard,
  Naked for greater shame,
He lies with fetters on each foot,
  Wrapt in a sheet of flame!

And all the while the burning lime
  Eats flesh and bone away,
It eats the brittle bone by night,
  And the soft flesh by day,
It eats the flesh and bone by turns
  But it eats the heart alway.

For three long years they will not sow
    Or root or seedling there:
For three long years the unblessed spot
    Will sterile be and bare,
And look upon the wondering sky
    With unreproachful stare.

They think a murderer's heart would taint
    Each simple seed they sow.
It is not true! God's kindly earth
    Is kindlier than men know,
And the red rose would but blow more red,
    The white rose whiter blow.

Out of his mouth a red, red rose!
    Out of his heart a white!
For who can say by what strange way
    Christ brings His will to light,
Since the barren staff the pilgrim bore
    Bloomed in the great Pope's sight?

But neither milk-white rose nor red
    May bloom in prison air;
The shard, the pebble, and the flint,
    Are what they give us there:
For flowers have been known to heal
    A common man's despair.

So never will wine-red rose or white,
    Petal by petal, fall
On that stretch of mud and sand that lies
    By the hideous prison wall,
To tell the men who tramp the yard
    That God's Son died for all.

PERCY FRENCH

1854–1920

71   From *The Queen's Afterdinner Speech*

(As overheard and Cut into Lengths of Poetry by Jamesy Murphy, Deputy-Assistant-Waiter at the Viceregal Lodge, A.D. 1901.)

'ME loving subjects,' sez she,
'Here's me best respects,' sez she,
'An' I'm proud this day,' sez she,
'Of the illigant way,' sez she,
'Ye gave me the hand,' sez she,
'Whin I came to land,' sez she,
'There was some people said,' sez she,
'They was greatly in dread,' sez she,
'I'd be moidhered or shot,' sez she,
'As like as not,' sez she.
'But 'tis mighty clear,' sez she,
''Tis not over here,' sez she,
'I have cause to fear,' sez she.
''Tis them Bulgruins,' sez she,
'That's throwing bombs,' sez she,
'And scaring the life,' sez she,
'Out of me son and the wife,' sez she.
'But in these parts,' sez she,
'They have warrum hearts,' sez she,
'And they like me well,' sez she,
'Barrin' Anna Parnell,' sez she,
'And that other wan,' sez she,
'That Maude Gonne,' sez she,
'Dhressin' in black,' sez she,
'To welcome me back,' sez she,

'Though I don't care,' sez she,
'What they wear,' sez she,
'An' all that gammon,' sez she,
'About me bringin' the famine,' sez she,
'Now Maude 'ill write,' sez she,
'That I brought the blight,' sez she,
'Or altered the saysons,' sez she,
'For political raysons,' sez she.
'An' I think there's a slate,' sez she,
'Off Willie Yeats,' sez she,
'He should be at home,' sez she,
'French polishin' a pome,' sez she,
'An' not writin' letters,' sez she,
'About his betters,' sez she,
'Paradin' me crimes,' sez she,
'In the *Irish Times*,' sez she. . . .

THOMAS WILLIAM ROLLESTON

1857–1920

72   *The Dead at Clonmacnoise*

(From the Irish)

IN a quiet water'd land, a land of roses,
    Stands Saint Kieran's city fair;
And the warriors of Erin in their famous generations
    Slumber there.

There beneath the dewy hillside sleep the noblest
    Of the clan of Conn,
Each below his stone with name in branching Ogham
    And the sacred knot thereon.

There they laid to rest the seven Kings of Tara,
   There the sons of Cairbré sleep—
Battle-banners of the Gael, that in Kieran's plain of crosses
   Now their final hosting keep.

And in Clonmacnoise they laid the men of Teffia,
   And right many a lord of Breagh;
Deep the sod above Clan Creidé and Clan Conaill,
   Kind in hall and fierce in fray.

Many and many a son of Conn, the Hundred-Fighter,
   In the red earth lies at rest;
Many a blue eye of Clan Colman the turf covers,
   Many a swan-white breast.

KUNO MEYER
1859–1919
(*Translations from the Irish*)

73   *The Crucifixion*

AT the cry of the first bird
They began to crucify Thee, O cheek like a swan
It were not right ever to cease lamenting—
It was like the parting of day from night.

Ah! though sore the suffering
Put upon the body of Mary's Son—
Sorer to Him was the grief
That was upon her for His sake.

74   *The Fort of Rathangan*

THE fort over against the oak-wood,
Once it was Bruidge's, it was Cathal's,
It was Aed's, it was Ailill's,
It was Conaing's, it was Cuilíne's
And it was Maeldúin's;
The fort remains after each in his turn—
And the kings asleep in the ground.

75   *The Deserted Home*

SADLY talks the blackbird here.
Well I know the woe he found:
No matter who cut down his nest,
For its young it was destroyed.

I myself not long ago
Found the woe he now has found.
Well I read thy song, O bird,
For the ruin of thy home.

Thy heart, O blackbird, burnt within
At the deed of reckless man:
Thy nest bereft of young and egg
The cowherd deems a trifling tale.

At thy clear notes they used to come,
Thy new-fledged children from afar;
No bird now comes from out thy house,
Across its edge the nettle grows.

They murdered them, the cowherd lads,
All thy children in one day:
One the fate to me and thee,
My own children live no more.

There was feeding by thy side
Thy mate, a bird from o'er the sea:
Then the snare entangled her,
At the cowherds hands she died.

O Thou, the Shaper of the world!
Uneven hands Thou layst on us:
Our fellows at our side are spared,
Their wives and children are alive.

A fairy host came as a blast
To bring destruction to our house:
Though bloodless was their taking off,
Yet dire as slaughter by the sword.

Woe for our wife, woe for our young!
The sadness of our grief is great:
No trace of them within, without—
And therefore is my heart so sad.

ELEANOR HULL
1860–1935

76 ### *The Soul's Desire*
(*From the Irish*)

IT were my soul's desire
    To see the face of God;
It were my soul's desire
    To rest in His abode.

It were my soul's desire
   To study zealously;
This, too, my soul's desire,
   A clear rule set for me.

It were my soul's desire
   A spirit free from gloom;
It were my soul's desire
   New life beyond the Doom.

It were my soul's desire
   To shun the chills of hell;
It were my soul's desire
   Within His house to dwell.

It were my soul's desire
   To imitate my King,
It were my soul's desire
   His ceaseless praise to sing.

It were my soul's desire,
   When heaven's gate is won,
To find my soul's desire
   Clear shining like the sun.

Grant, Lord, my soul's desire,
   Deep waves of cleansing sighs;
Grant, Lord, my soul's desire
   From earthly cares to rise.

This still my soul's desire—
   Whatever life afford—
To gain my soul's desire
   And see Thy face, O Lord.

KATHERINE TYNAN

1861–1931

77   *A Memory*

THIS is just the weather, a wet May and blowing,
   All the shining, shimmering leaves tossing low and high,
When my father used to say: "Twill be the great mowing!
   God's weather's a good weather, be it wet or dry.'

Blue were his eyes and his cheeks were so ruddy,
   He was out in all weathers, up and down the farm;
With the pleasant smile and the word for a wet body;
   'Sure, the weather's God's weather. Who can take the
      harm?'

With a happy word he'd silence all repining
   While the hay lay wet in field and the cattle died,
When the rain rained every day and no sun was shining:
   'Ah, well, God is good,' he'd say, even while he sighed.

In the parched summer with the corn not worth saving,
   Every field bare as your hand and the beasts to feed,
Still he kept his heart up, while other folk were raving:
   'God will send the fodder: 'tis He that knows the need.'

A wet May, a wild May; he used to rise up cheery
   In the grey of the morning for market and for fair.
Now he sleeps the whole year long, though days be bright,
      be dreary,
   In God's weather that's good weather he sleeps without
      a care.

Now, 'tis just the weather, a wild May and weeping,
    How the blackbird sang and sang 'mid the tossing leaves!
When my father used to say: "Twill be the great reaping:
    God send fine weather to carry home the sheaves!'

78   *Lux in Tenebris*

AT night what things will stalk abroad,
    What veilèd shapes and eyes of dread!
With phantoms in a lonely road
    And visions of the dead.

The kindly room when day is here,
    At night takes ghostly terrors on;
And every shadow hath its fear,
    And every wind its moan.

Lord Jesus, Day-Star of the world,
    Rise Thou, and bid this dark depart,
And all the east, a rose uncurled,
    Grow golden at the heart!

Lord, in the watches of the night,
    Keep Thou my soul! a trembling thing
As any moth that in daylight
    Will spread a rainbow wing.

79   *The Making of Birds*

GOD made Him birds in a pleasant humour;
    Tired of planets and suns was He.
He said: 'I will add a glory to Summer,
    Gifts for my creatures banished from Me!'

He had a thought and it set Him smiling
  Of the shape of a bird and its glancing head,
Its dainty air and its grace beguiling:
  'I will make feathers,' the Lord God said.

He made the robin; He made the swallow;
  His deft hands moulding the shape to His mood,
The thrush and lark and the finch to follow,
  And laughed to see that His work was good.

He Who has given men gift of laughter—
  Made in His image; He fashioned fit
The blink of the owl and the stork thereafter,
  The little wren and the long-tailed tit.

He spent in the making His wit and fancies;
  The wing-feathers He fashioned them strong;
Deft and dear as daisies and pansies,
  He crowned His work with the gift of song.

'Dearlings', He said, 'make songs for My praises!'
  He tossed them loose to the sun and wind,
Airily sweet as pansies and daisies;
  He taught them to build a nest to their mind.

The dear Lord God of His glories weary—
  Christ our Lord had the heart of a boy—
Made Him birds in a moment merry,
  Bade them soar and sing for His joy.

80   *Sheep and Lambs*

ALL in the April evening,
  April airs were abroad,
The sheep with their little lambs
  Passed me by on the road.

The sheep with their little lambs
  Passed me by on the road;
All in the April evening
  I thought on the Lamb of God.

The lambs were weary, and crying
  With a weak, human cry.
I thought on the Lamb of God
  Going meekly to die.

Up in the blue, blue mountains
  Dewy pastures are sweet;
Rest for the little bodies,
  Rest for the little feet,

But for the Lamb of God,
  Up on the hilltop green,
Only a cross of shame
  Two stark crosses between.

All in the April evening,
  April airs were abroad;
I saw the sheep with their lambs,
  And thought on the Lamb of God.

FRANCIS CARLIN

1861–1945

81   *Ballad of Douglas Bridge*

On Douglas Bridge I met a man
Who lived adjacent to Strabane,
  Before the English hung him high
For riding with O'Hanlon.

The eyes of him were just as fresh
As when they burned within the flesh;
   And his boot-legs were wide apart
From riding with O'Hanlon.

'God save you, Sir,' I said with fear,
'You seem to be a stranger here.'
   'Not I,' said he, 'nor any man
Who rides with Count O'Hanlon.

'I know each glen from North Tyrone
To Monaghan, and I've been known
   By every clan and parish since
Irode with Count O'Hanlon.

'Before that time,' said he to me,
'My fathers owned the land you see;
   But they are now among the moors
A-riding with O'Hanlon.

'Before that time,' said he with pride,
'My fathers rode where now they ride
   As Rapparees, before the time
Of trouble and O'Hanlon.

'Good night to you, and God be with
The tellers of the tale and myth,
   For they are of the spirit-stuff
That rides with Count O'Hanlon.'

Good night to you,' said I, 'and God
Be with the chargers, fairy-shod,
   That bear the Ulster heroes forth
To ride with Count O'Hanlon.'

On Douglas Bridge we parted, but
The Gap o' Dreams is never shut
To one whose saddled soul to-night
Rides out with Count O'Hanlon.

DOUGLAS HYDE
1862–1946

(*Translations from the Irish*)

82 ## *My Grief on the Sea*

MY grief on the sea,
How the waves of it roll!
For they heave between me
And the love of my soul!

Abandoned, forsaken,
To grief and to care,
Will the sea ever waken
Relief from despair?

My grief, and my trouble!
Would he and I were
In the province of Leinster,
Or county of Clare.

Were I and my darling—
Oh, heart-bitter wound!—
On board of the ship
For America bound.

On a green bed of rushes
All last night I lay,
And I flung it abroad
With the heat of the day.

And my love came behind me—
He came from the south;
His breast to my bosom,
His mouth to my mouth.

83   *Ringleted Youth of My Love*

RINGLETED youth of my love,
With thy locks bound loosely behind thee,
You passed by the road above,
But you never came in to find me;
Where were the harm for you
If you came for a little to see me,
Your kiss is a wakening dew
Were I ever so ill or so dreamy.

If I had golden store
I would make a nice little boreen,
To lead straight up to his door,
The door of the house of my storeen;
Hoping to God not to miss
The sound of his footfall in it,
I have waited so long for his kiss
That for days I have slept not a minute.

I thought, O my love! you were so—
As the moon is, or sun on a fountain,
And I thought after that you were snow,
The cold snow on top of the mountain;

126

And I thought after that, you were more
Like God's lamp shining to find me,
Or the bright star of knowledge before,
And the star of knowledge behind me.

You promised me high-heeled shoes,
And satin and silk, my storeen,
And to follow me, never to lose,
Though the ocean were round us roaring
Like a bush in a gap in a wall
I am now left lonely without thee,
And this house I grow dead of, is all
That I see around or about me.

84   *The Mystery*

I AM the wind which breathes upon the sea,
I am the wave of the ocean,
I am the murmur of the billows,
I am the ox of the seven combats,
I am the vulture upon the rocks,
I am a beam of the sun,
I am the fairest of plants,
I am a wild boar in valour,
I am a salmon in the water,
I am a lake in the plain,
I am a word of science,
I am the point of the lance of battle,
I am the God who created in the head the fire.
Who is it that throws light into the meeting on the
        mountain?
Who announces the ages of the moon?
Who teaches the place where couches the sun?
                                        (If not I)

The Red Man's Wife

'Tis what they say,
Thy little heel fits in a shoe.
'Tis what they say,
Thy little mouth kisses well, too.
'Tis what they say,
Thousand loves that you leave me to rue;
That the tailor went the way
That the wife of the Red man knew.

Nine months did I spend
In a prison penned tightly and bound;
Bolts on my smalls
And a thousand locks frowning around;
But o'er the tide
I would leap with the leap of a swan,
Could I once set my side
By the bride of the Red-haired man.

I thought, O my life,
That one house between us, love, would be;
And I thought I should find
You once coaxing my child on your knee;
But now the curse of the High One,
On him let it be,
And on all of the band of the liars
Who put silence between you and me.

There grows a tree in the garden
With blossoms that tremble and shake,
I lay my hands on its bark
And I feel that my heart must break.

On one wish alone
My soul through the long months ran,
One little kiss
From the wife of the Red-haired man.

But the day of doom shall come,
And hills and harbours be rent;
A mist shall fall on the sun
From the dark clouds heavily sent;
The sea shall be dry,
And earth under mourning and ban;
Then loud shall he cry
For the wife of the Red-haired man.

86   *I Shall not Die for Thee*

FOR thee I shall not die,
Woman high of fame and name;
Foolish men thou mayest slay,
I and they are not the same.

Why should I expire
For the fire of any eye,
Slender waist or swan-like limb,
Is't for them that I should die?

The round breasts, the fresh skin,
Cheeks crimson, hair like silk to touch,
Indeed, indeed, I shall not die,
Please God, not I for any such!

The golden locks, the forehead thin,
The quiet mien, the gracious ease,
The rounded heel, the languid tone,
Fools alone find death from these.

Thy sharp wit, thy perfect calm,
Thy thin palm like foam of the sea;
Thy white neck, thy blue eye,
I shall not die for thee.

Woman, graceful as the swan,
A wise man did rear me too,
Little palm, white neck, bright eye,
I shall not die for you.

W. B. YEATS

1865–1939

87 *The Stolen Child*

WHERE dips the rocky highland
Of Sleuth Wood in the lake,
There lies a leafy island
Where flapping herons wake
The drowsy water-rats;
There we've hid our faery vats,
Full of berries
And of reddest stolen cherries.
Come away, O human child!
To the waters and the wild
With a faery, hand in hand,
For the world's more full of weeping than
 you can understand.

Where the wave of moonlight glosses
The dim grey sands with light,
Far off by furthest Rosses
We foot it all the night,

Weaving olden dances,
Mingling hands and mingling glances
Till the moon has taken flight;
To and fro we leap
And chase the frothy bubbles,
While the world is full of troubles
And is anxious in its sleep.
Come away, O human child!
To the waters and the wild
With a faery, hand in hand,
For the world's more full of weeping than
*   you can understand.*

Where the wandering water gushes
From the hills above Glen-Car,
In pools among the rushes
That scarce could bathe a star,
We seek for slumbering trout
And whispering in their ears
Give them unquiet dreams;
Leaning softly out
From ferns that drop their tears
Over the young streams.
Come away, O human child!
To the waters and the wild
With a faery, hand in hand,
For the world's more full of weeping than
*   you can understand.*

Away with us he's going,
The solemn-eyed:
He'll hear no more the lowing
Of the calves on the warm hillside

Or the kettle on the hob
Sing peace into his breast,
Or see the brown mice bob
Round and round the oatmeal-chest.
For he comes, the human child,
To the waters and the wild
With a faery, hand in hand,
From a world more full of weeping than
he can understand.

88   *Down by the Salley Gardens*

DOWN by the salley gardens my love and I did meet;
She passed the salley gardens with little snow-white feet.
She bid me take love easy, as the leaves grow on the tree;
But I, being young and foolish, with her would not agree.

In a field by the river my love and I did stand,
And on my leaning shoulder she laid her snow-white hand.
She bid me take life easy, as the grass grows on the weirs;
But I was young and foolish, and now am full of tears.

89   *To Ireland in the Coming Times*

KNOW, that I would accounted be
True brother of a company
That sang, to sweeten Ireland's wrong,
Ballad and story, rann[1] and song;
Nor be I any less of them,
Because the red-rose-bordered hem

[1] *Rann*: a quatrain, verse, or stanza.

Of her, whose history began
Before God made the angelic clan,
Trails all about the written page.
When Time began to rant and rage
The measure of her flying feet
Made Ireland's heart begin to beat;
And Time bade all his candles flare
To light a measure here and there;
And may the thoughts of Ireland brood
Upon a measured quietude.

Nor may I less be counted one
With Davis, Mangan, Ferguson,
Because, to him who ponders well,
My rhymes more than their rhyming tell
Of things discovered in the deep,
Where only body's laid asleep.
For the elemental creatures go
About my table to and fro,
That hurry from unmeasured mind
To rant and rage in flood and wind;
Yet he who treads in measured ways
May surely barter gaze for gaze.
Man ever journeys on with them
After the red-rose-bordered hem.
Ah, faeries, dancing under the moon,
A Druid land, a Druid tune!

While still I may, I write for you
The love I lived, the dream I knew.
From our birthday, until we die,
Is but the winking of an eye;
And we, our singing and our love,
What measurer Time has lit above,

And all benighted things that go
About my table to and fro,
Are passing on to where may be,
In truth's consuming ecstasy,
No place for love and dream at all;
For God goes by with white footfall.
I cast my heart into my rhymes,
That you, in the dim coming times,
May know how my heart went with them
After the red-rose-bordered hem.

90   *Red Hanrahan's Song About Ireland*

THE old brown thorn-trees break in two high over Cum-
    men Strand,
Under a bitter black wind that blows from the left hand;
Our courage breaks like an old tree in a black wind and dies,
But we have hidden in our hearts the flame out of the eyes
Of Cathleen, the daughter of Houlihan.

The wind has bundled up the clouds high over Knock-
    narea,
And thrown the thunder on the stones for all that Maeve
    can say.
Angers that are like noisy clouds have set our hearts abeat;
But we have all bent low and low and kissed the quiet feet
Of Cathleen, the daughter of Houlihan.

The yellow pool has overflowed high up on Clooth-na-
    Bare,
For the wet winds are blowing out of the clinging air;
Like heavy flooded waters our bodies and our blood;
But purer than a tall candle before the Holy Rood
Is Cathleen, the daughter of Houlihan.

91

Easter 1916

I HAVE met them at close of day
Coming with vivid faces
From counter or desk among grey
Eighteenth-century houses.
I have passed with a nod of the head
Or polite meaningless words,
Or have lingered awhile and said
Polite meaningless words,
And thought before I had done
Of a mocking tale or a gibe
To please a companion
Around the fire at the club,
Being certain that they and I
But lived where motley is worn:
All changed, changed utterly:
A terrible beauty is born.

That woman's days were spent
In ignorant good-will,
Her nights in argument
Until her voice grew shrill.
What voice more sweet than hers
When, young and beautiful,
She rode to harriers?
This man had kept a school
And rode our wingèd horse;
This other his helper and friend
Was coming into his force;
He might have won fame in the end,

So sensitive his nature seemed,
So daring and sweet his thought.
This other man I had dreamed
A drunken, vainglorious lout.
He had done most bitter wrong
To some who are near my heart,
Yet I number him in the song;
He, too, has resigned his part
In the casual comedy;
He, too, has been changed in his turn,
Transformed utterly:
A terrible beauty is born.

Hearts with one purpose alone
Through summer and winter seem
Enchanted to a stone
To trouble the living stream.
The horse that comes from the road,
The rider, the birds that range
From cloud to tumbling cloud,
Minute by minute they change;
A shadow of cloud on the stream
Changes minute by minute;
A horse-hoof slides on the brim,
And a horse plashes within it;
The long-legged moor-hens dive,
And hens to moor-cocks call;
Minute by minute they live:
The stone's in the midst of all.

Too long a sacrifice
Can make a stone of the heart.
O when may it suffice?
That is Heaven's part, our part

To murmur name upon name,
As a mother names her child
When sleep at last has come
On limbs that had run wild.
What is it but nightfall?
No, no, not night but death;
Was it needless death after all?
For England may keep faith
For all that is done and said.
We know their dream; enough
To know they dreamed and are dead;
And what if excess of love
Bewildered them till they died?
I write it out in a verse—
MacDonagh and MacBride
And Connolly and Pearse
Now and in time to be,
Wherever green is worn,
Are changed, changed utterly:
A terrible beauty is born.

92 *In Memory of Eva Gore-Booth and Con Markiewicz*

THE light of evening, Lissadell,
Great windows open to the south,
Two girls in silk kimonos, both
Beautiful, one a gazelle.
But a raving autumn shears
Blossom from the summer's wreath;
The older is condemned to death,
Pardoned, drags out lonely years

Conspiring among the ignorant.
I know not what the younger dreams—
Some vague Utopia—and she seems,
When withered old and skeleton-gaunt,
An image of such politics.
Many a time I think to seek
One or the other out and speak
Of that old Georgian mansion, mix
Pictures of the mind, recall
That table and the talk of youth,
Two girls in silk kimonos, both
Beautiful, one a gazelle.

Dear shadows, now you know it all,
All the folly of a fight
With a common wrong or right.
The innocent and the beautiful
Have no enemy but time;
Arise and bid me strike a match
And strike another till time catch;
Should the conflagration climb,
Run till all the sages know.
We the great gazebo built,
They convicted us of guilt;
Bid me strike a match and blow.

93   *The Second Coming*

TURNING and turning in the widening gyre
The falcon cannot hear the falconer;
Things fall apart; the centre cannot hold;
Mere anarchy is loosed upon the world,

The blood-dimmed tide is loosed, and everywhere
The ceremony of innocence is drowned;
The best lack all conviction, while the worst
Are full of passionate intensity.

Surely some revelation is at hand;
Surely the Second Coming is at hand.
The Second Coming! Hardly are those words out
When a vast image out of *Spiritus Mundi*
Troubles my sight: somewhere in sands of the desert
A shape with lion body and the head of a man,
A gaze blank and pitiless as the sun,
Is moving its slow thighs, while all about it
Reel shadows of the indignant desert birds.
The darkness drops again; but now I know
That twenty centuries of stony sleep
Were vexed to nightmare by a rocking cradle,
And what rough beast, its hour come round at last,
Slouches towards Bethlehem to be born?

94   *Sailing to Byzantium*

I

THAT is no country for old men. The young
In one another's arms, birds in the trees,
—Those dying generations—at their song,
The salmon-falls, the mackerel-crowded seas,
Fish, flesh, or fowl, commend all summer long
Whatever is begotten, born, and dies.
Caught in that sensual music all neglect
Monuments of unageing intellect.

II

An aged man is but a paltry thing,
A tattered coat upon a stick, unless
Soul clap its hands and sing, and louder sing
For every tatter in its mortal dress,
Nor is there singing school but studying
Monuments of its own magnificence;
And therefore I have sailed the seas and come
To the holy city of Byzantium.

III

O sages standing in God's holy fire
As in the gold mosaic of a wall,
Come from the holy fire, perne in a gyre,
And be the singing-masters of my soul.
Consume my heart away; sick with desire
And fastened to a dying animal
It knows not what it is; and gather me
Into the artifice of eternity.

IV

Once out of nature I shall never take
My bodily form from any natural thing,
But such a form as Grecian goldsmiths make
Of hammered gold and gold enamelling
To keep a drowsy Emperor awake;
Or set upon a golden bough to sing
To lords and ladies of Byzantium
Of what is past, or passing, or to come.

95   *Coole Park, 1929*

I MEDITATE upon a swallow's flight,
Upon an aged woman and her house,
A sycamore and lime-tree lost in night
Although that western cloud is luminous,
Great works constructed there in nature's spite
For scholars and for poets after us,
Thoughts long knitted into a single thought,
A dance-like glory that those walls begot.

There Hyde before he had beaten into prose
That noble blade the Muses buckled on,
There one that ruffled in a manly pose
For all his timid heart, there that slow man,
That meditative man, John Synge, and those
Impetuous men, Shawe-Taylor and Hugh Lane
Found pride established in humility,
A scene well set and excellent company.

They came like swallows and like swallows went,
And yet a woman's powerful character
Could keep a swallow to its first intent;
And half a dozen in formation there,
That seemed to whirl upon a compass-point,
Found certainty upon the dreaming air,
The intellectual sweetness of those lines
That cut through time or cross it withershins.

Here, traveller, scholar, poet, take your stand
When all those rooms and passages are gone,
When nettles wave upon a shapeless mound
And saplings root among the broken stone,

And dedicate—eyes bent upon the ground,
Back turned upon the brightness of the sun
And all the sensuality of the shade—
A moment's memory to that laurelled head.

96   *Under Ben Bulben*

I

SWEAR by what the sages spoke
Round the Mareotic Lake
That the Witch of Atlas knew,
Spoke and set the cocks a-crow.

Swear by those horsemen, by those women
Complexion and form prove superhuman,
That pale, long-visaged company
That air in immortality
Completeness of their passions won;
Now they ride the wintry dawn
Where Ben Bulben sets the scene.

Here's the gist of what they mean.

II

Many times man lives and dies
Between his two eternities,
That of race and that of soul,
And ancient Ireland knew it all.
Whether man die in his bed
Or the rifle knocks him dead,
A brief parting from those dear
Is the worst man has to fear.

Though grave-diggers' toil is long,
Sharp their spades, their muscles strong,
They but thrust their buried men
Back in the human mind again.

III

You that Mitchel's prayer have heard,
'Send war in our time, O Lord!'
Know that when all words are said
And a man is fighting mad,
Something drops from eyes long blind,
He completes his partial mind,
For an instant stands at ease,
Laughs aloud, his heart at peace.
Even the wisest man grows tense
With some sort of violence
Before he can accomplish fate,
Know his work or choose his mate.

IV

Poet and sculptor, do the work,
Nor let the modish painter shirk
What his great forefathers did,
Bring the soul of man to God,
Make him fill the cradles right.

Measurement began our might:
Forms a stark Egyptian thought,
Forms that gentler Phidias wrought.
Michael Angelo left a proof
On the Sistine Chapel roof,
Where but half-awakened Adam
Can disturb globe-trotting Madam

Till her bowels are in heat,
Proof that there's a purpose set
Before the secret working mind:
Profane perfection of mankind.

Quattrocento put in paint
On backgrounds for a God or Saint
Gardens where a soul's at ease;
Where everything that meets the eye,
Flowers and grass and cloudless sky,
Resemble forms that are or seem
When sleepers wake and yet still dream,
And when it's vanished still declare,
With only bed and bedstead there,
That heavens had opened.
                              Gyres run on;
When that greater dream had gone
Calvert and Wilson, Blake and Claude,
Prepared a rest for the people of God,
Palmer's phrase, but after that
Confusion fell upon our thought.

V

Irish poets, learn your trade,
Sing whatever is well made,
Scorn the sort now growing up
All out of shape from toe to top,
Their unremembering hearts and heads
Base-born products of base beds.
Sing the peasantry, and then
Hard-riding country gentlemen,
The holiness of monks, and after
Porter-drinkers' randy laughter;

Sing the lords and ladies gay
That were beaten into the clay
Through seven heroic centuries;
Cast your mind on other days
That we in coming days may be
Still the indomitable Irishry.

VI

Under bare Ben Bulben's head
In Drumcliff churchyard Yeats is laid.
An ancestor was rector there
Long years ago, a church stands near,
By the road an ancient cross.
No marble, no conventional phrase;
On limestone quarried near the spot
By his command these words are cut:

> *Cast a cold eye*
> *On life, on death.*
> *Horseman, pass by!*

HERBERT TRENCH

1865–1923

97   *Jean Richepin's Song*

I

A POOR lad once and a lad so trim,
  (*Fol de rol de raly O!*
    Fol de rol!)
A poor lad once and a lad so trim
Gave his love to her that loved not him.

II

And, says she, 'Fetch me tonight, you rogue,'
   (*Fol de rol de raly O!*
     Fol de rol!)
And, says she, 'Fetch me tonight, you rogue,
Your mother's heart to feed my dog!'

III

To his mother's house went that young man,
   (*Fol de rol de raly O!*
     Fol de rol!)
To his mother's house went that young man,
Killed her, and took the heart, and ran.

IV

And as he was running, look you, he fell,
   (*Fol de rol de raly O!*
     Fol de rol!)
And as he was running, look you, he fell,
And the heart rolled on the ground as well.

V

And the lad, as the heart was a-rolling, heard
   (*Fol de rol de raly, O!*
     Fol de rol!)
And the lad, as the heart was a-rolling, heard
That the heart was speaking, and this was the word—

VI

The heart was a-weeping, and crying so small
   (*Fol de rol de raly O!*
     Fol de rol!)
The heart was a-weeping and crying so small,
'Are you hurt, my child, are you hurt at all?'

PHILIP FRANCIS LITTLE

1866–1926

The Three Poplars

I SHALL have three grey poplar trees above me when I
      sleep;
the poplars will not sway or swing, nor like the willow
      weep,
but upright as the staff of one who watcheth o'er his sheep.

Some fount may open silvern lips near by; not far away
the harvester his voice may lift in solemn joy; three grey
great poplars will refresh him with their shade in the noon-
      day.

And when to every creature Night repose and respite
      brings,
profound my sleep, the while to me the dew-wet meadow
      clings,
soft garment of the Poor, which is the cerecloth, too, of
      Kings.

As when the Shadow Hand of Eventide the toiling Bee
at last will homeward guide, and guide unto her sheltering
      tree
the weary singing Bird, so may the kind night come for
      me!

I shall have three grey poplar trees above me when I sleep;
the poplars will not sway or swing, nor like the willow
      weep,
but upright as the staff of one who watcheth o'er his sheep.

DORA SIGERSON SHORTER

1866–1917

99   *The Kine of My Father*

THE kine of my father, they are straying from my keeping;
    The young goat's at mischief, but little can I do:
For all through the night did I hear the banshee keening;
    O youth of my loving, and is it well with you?

All through the night sat my mother with my sorrow;
    'Wisht, it is the storm, O one childeen of my heart!'
My hair with the wind, and my two hands clasped in
      anguish;
    Black head of my darling! too long are we apart.

Were your grave at my feet, I would think it half a blessing;
    I could herd then the cattle, and drive the goats away;
Many a Paternoster I would say for your safe keeping;
    I could sleep above your heart until the dawn of day.

I see you on the prairie, hot with thirst and faint with
      hunger,
    The head that I love lying low upon the sand.
The vultures shriek impatient, the coyote dogs are howling,
Till the blood is pulsing cold within your clenching hand.

I see you on the waters, so white, so still, forsaken,
    Your dear eyes unclosing beneath a foreign rain:
A plaything of the winds, you turn and drift unceasing;
    No grave for your resting; Oh, mine the bitter pain!

148

All through the night did I hear the banshee keening:
  Somewhere you are dying, and nothing can I do:
My hair with the wind, and my two hands clasped in
    anguish;
  Bitter is your trouble—and I am far from you.

100   *Ireland*

'Twas the dream of a God,
  And the mould of His hand,
That you shook 'neath His stroke,
That you trembled and broke
  To this beautiful land.

Here He loosed from His hold
  A brown tumult of wings,
Till the wind on the sea
Bore the strange melody
  Of an island that sings.

He made you all fair,
  You in purple and gold,
You in silver and green,
Till no eye that has seen
  Without love can behold.

I have left you behind
  In the path of the past,
With the white breath of flowers,
With the best of God's hours,
  I have left you at last.

149

ETHNA CARBERY

1866–1902

The Love-Talker

I MET the Love-Talker one eve in the glen,
He was handsomer than any of our handsome young men,
His eyes were blacker than the sloe, his voice sweeter far
Than the crooning of old Kevin's pipes beyond in Cool-
nagar.

I was bound for the milking with a heart fair and free—
My grief! my grief! that bitter hour drained the life from
me;
I thought him human lover, though his lips on mine were
cold,
And the breath of death blew keen on me within his hold.

I know not what way he came, no shadow fell behind,
But all the sighing rushes swayed beneath a fairy wind;
The thrush ceased its singing, a mist crept about,
We two clung together—with the world shut out.

Beyond the ghostly mist I could hear my cattle low,
The little cow from Ballina, clean as driven snow,
The dun cow from Kerry, the roan from Inisheer,
Oh, pitiful their calling—and his whispers in my ear!

His eyes were a fire; his words were a snare;
I cried my mother's name, but no help was there;
I made the blessed Sign—then he gave a dreary moan,
A wisp of cloud went floating by, and I stood alone.

Running ever thro' my head is an old-time rune—
'Who meets the Love-Talker must weave her shroud
    soon.'
My mother's face is furrowed with the salt tears that fall,
But the kind eyes of my father are the saddest sight of all.

I have spun the fleecy lint and now my wheel is still,
The linen length is woven for my shroud fine and chill,
I shall stretch me on the bed where a happy maid I lay—
Pray for the soul of Máire Óg at dawning of the day!

Æ. (GEORGE W. RUSSELL)

1867–1935

102   *Reconciliation*

I BEGIN through the grass once again to be bound to the
    Lord;
I can see, through a face that has faded, the face full of rest
Of the earth, of the mother, my heart with her heart in
    accord,
As I lie 'mid the cool green tresses that mantle her breast
I begin with the grass once again to be bound to the Lord.

By the hand of a child I am led to the throne of the King
For a touch that now fevers me not is forgotten and far,
And His infinite sceptred hands that sway us can bring
Me in dreams from the laugh of a child to the song of a
    star.
On the laugh of a child I am borne to the joy of the King.

103 *The Outcast*

SOMETIMES when alone
At the dark close of day,
Men meet an outlawed majesty
And hurry away.

They come to the lighted house;
They talk to their dear;
They crucify the mystery
With words of good cheer.

When love and life are over,
And flight's at an end,
On the outcast majesty
They lean as a friend.

104 *The Great Breath*

ITS edges foamed with amethyst and rose,
Withers once more the old blue flower of day:
There where the ether like a diamond glows
   Its petals fade away.

A shadowy tumult stirs the dusky air;
Sparkle the delicate dews, the distant snows;
The great deep thrills, for through it everywhere
   The breath of Beauty blows.

I saw how all the trembling ages past,
Moulded to her by deep and deeper breath,
Neared to the hour when Beauty breathes her last
   And knows herself in death.

THOMAS BOYD
1867–1927

The King's Son

WHO rideth through the driving rain
　　At such a headlong speed?
Naked and pale he rides amain
　　Upon a naked steed.

Nor hollow nor height his going bars,
　　His wet steed shines like silk,
His head is golden to the stars
　　And his limbs are white as milk.

But, lo, he dwindles as a light
　　That lifts from a black mere,
And, as the fair youth wanes from sight,
　　The steed grows mightier.

What wizard by yon holy tree
　　Mutters unto the sky
Where Macha's flame-tongued horses flee
　　On hooves of thunder by?

Ah, 'tis not holy so to ban
　　The youth of kingly seed:
Ah! woe, the wasting of a man
　　Who changes to a steed.

Nightly upon the Plain of Kings
　　When Macha's day is nigh
He gallops; and the dark wind brings
　　His lonely human cry.

Love on the Mountain

My love comes down from the mountain
  Through the mists of dawn;
I look, and the star of the morning
  From the sky is gone.

My love comes down from the mountain,
  At dawn, dewy-sweet;
Did you step from the star to the mountain,
  O little white feet?

O whence came your twining tresses
  And your shining eyes,
But out of the gold of the morning
  And the blue of the skies?

The misty mountain is burning
  In the sun's red fire,
And the heart in my breast is burning
  And lost in desire.

I follow you into the valley
  But no word can I say;
To the East or the West I will follow
  Till the dusk of my day.

NORA HOPPER
1871–1906

'Tis I go Fiddling, Fiddling

'TIS I go fiddling, fiddling,
  By weedy ways forlorn:
I make the blackbird's music
  Ere in his breast 'tis born:
The sleeping larks I waken
  Twixt the midnight and the morn.

No man alive has seen me,
  But women hear me play
Sometimes at door or window,
  Fiddling the souls away,—
The child's soul and the colleen's
  Out of the covering clay.

None of my fairy kinsmen
  Make music with me now:
Alone the raths I wander
  Or ride the whitethorn bough
But the wild swans they know me,
  And the horse that draws the plough.

JOHN MILLINGTON SYNGE
1871–1909

Beg-Innish

BRING Kateen-Beag and Maurya Jude
To dance in Beg-Innish,
And when the lads (they're in Dunquin)
Have sold their crabs and fish,

155

Wave fawney shawls and call them in,
And call the little girls who spin,
And seven weavers from Dunquin,
To dance in Beg-Innish.

I'll play you jigs, and Maurice Kean,
Where nets are laid to dry,
I've silken strings would draw a dance
From girls are lame or shy;
Four strings I've brought from Spain and France
To make your long men skip and prance,
Till stars look out to see the dance
Where nets are laid to dry.

We'll have no priest or peeler in
To dance at Beg-Innish;
But we'll have drink from M'riarty Jim
Rowed round while gannets fish,
A keg with porter to the brim,
That every lad may have his whim,
Till we up with sails with M'riarty Jim
And sail from Beg-Innish.

109   *To the Oaks of Glencree*

My arms are round you, and I lean
Against you, while the lark
Sings over us, and golden lights and green
Shadows are on your bark.

There'll come a season when you'll stretch
Black boards to cover me;
Then in Mount Jerome I'll lie, poor wretch,
With worms eternally.

110 *A Question*

I ASKED if I got sick and died, would you
With my black funeral go walking too,
If you'd stand close to hear them talk or pray
While I'm let down in that steep bank of clay.

And, No, you said, for if you saw a crew
Of living idiots pressing round that new
Oak coffin—they alive, I dead beneath
That board—you'd rave and rend them with your teeth.

111 *In Glencullen*

THRUSH, linnet, stare, and wren,
Brown lark beside the sun,
Take thought of kestrel, sparrow-hawk,
Birdlime and roving gun.

You great-great-grandchildren
Of birds I've listened to,
I think I robbed your ancestors
When I was young as you.

112 From *The Playboy of the Western
World*

CHRISTY [*indignantly*] Starting from you is it? I will not,
then, and when the airs is warming, in four months or
five, it's then yourself and me should be pacing Neifin
in the dews of night, the times sweet smells do be rising,
and you'd see a little, shiny new moon, maybe sinking
on the hills.

PEGEEN [*looking at him playfully*] And it's that kind of a poacher's love you'd make, Christy Mahon, on the sides of Neifin, when the night is down?

CHRISTY. It's little you'll think if my love's a poacher's, or an earl's itself, when you'll feel my two hands stretched around you, and I squeezing kisses on your puckered lips, till I'd feel a kind of pity for the Lord God is all ages sitting lonesome in His golden chair.

PEGEEN. That'll be right fun, Christy Mahon, and any girl would walk her heart out before she'd meet a young man was your like for eloquence, or talk at all.

CHRISTY [*encouraged*] Let you wait to hear me talking till we're astray in Erris, when Good Friday's by, drinking a sup from a well, and making mighty kisses with our wetted mouths, or gaming in a gap of sunshine, with yourself stretched back unto your necklace, in the flowers of the earth.

PEGEEN [*in a low voice, moved by his tone*] I'd be nice so, is it?

CHRISTY [*with rapture*] If the mitred bishops seen you that time, they'd be the like of the holy prophets I'm thinking, do be straining the bars of paradise to lay eyes on the Lady Helen of Troy, and she abroad pacing back and forward with a nosegay in her golden shawl.

PEGEEN [*with real tenderness*] And what is it I have, Christy Mahon, to make me fitting entertainment for the like of you, that has such poet's talking and such bravery of heart?

CHRISTY [*in a low voice*] Isn't there the light of seven heavens in your heart alone the way you'll be an angel's lamp to me from this out, and I abroad in the darkness spearing salmons in the Owen or the Carrowmore?

PEGEEN. If I was your wife I'd be along with you those nights, Christy Mahon, the way you'd see I was a great hand at coaxing bailiffs, or coining funny nicknames for the stars of night.

CHRISTY. You is it? Taking your death in the hailstones or in the fogs of dawn.

PEGEEN. Yourself and me would shelter easy in a narrow bush [*with a qualm of dread*]; but we're only talking, maybe, for this would be a poor, thatched place to hold a fine lad is the like of you.

CHRISTY [*putting his arm around her*] If I wasn't a good Christian it's on my naked knees I'd be saying my prayers and paters to every jackstraw you have roofing your head, and every stony pebble is paving the laneway to your door.

PEGEEN [*radiantly*] If that's the truth I'll be burning candles from this out to the miracles of God that have brought you from the South to-day and I with my gowns bought ready, the way that I can wed you, and not wait at all.

CHRISTY. It's miracles and that's the truth. Me there toiling a long while and walking a long while not knowing at all I was drawing all times nearer to this holy day.

PEGEEN. And myself a girl was tempted to go sailing the seas till I'd marry a Jewman with ten kegs of gold, and I not knowing at all there was the like of you drawing nearer, like the stars of God.

CHRISTY. And to think I'm long years hearing women talking that talk to all bloody fools, and this the first time I've heard the like of your voice talking sweetly for my own delight.

PEGEEN. And to think it's me is talking sweetly, Christy Mahon, and I the fright of seven townlands for my biting tongue. Well, the heart's a wonder; and I'm thinking there won't be our like in Mayo for gallant lovers from this hour today. (*From Act III*)

JAMES H. COUSINS

1873–1955

113   *High and Low*

HE stumbled home from Clifden fair
With drunken song, and cheeks aglow.
Yet there was something in his air
That told of kingship long ago.
I sighed—and inly cried
With grief that one so high should fall so low.

He snatched a flower and sniffed its scent,
And waved it toward the sunset sky.
Some old sweet rapture through him went
And kindled in his bloodshot eye.
I turned—and inly burned
With joy that one so low should rise so high.

114   *Behind the Plough*

BLACK wings and white in the hollow
Follow the track of the team,
While the sun from the noon declining
Is shining on toil-wet brows.
Birds of the mountain and sea-birds
Circle and swoop and scream,
Searching for spoils of the furrow
Where slowly the ploughman ploughs.

Make me room, O birds! I am sweeping
From the Boughs of Sleeping afar;
I have winged thro' the mists of the ages,
Where sages drone and drowse;
I follow the feet of the Horses
That drag the Morning Star,
To search in the spoils of the furrow,
Where God the Ploughman ploughs.

THOMAS MacDONAGH
1878–1916

115 *John-John*

I DREAMT last night of you, John-John,
   And thought you called to me;
And when I woke this morning, John,
   Yourself I hoped to see;
But I was all alone, John-John,
   Though still I heard your call:
I put my boots and bonnet on,
   And took my Sunday shawl,
And went, full sure to find you, John,
          To Nenagh fair.

The fair was just the same as then,
   Five years ago to-day,
When first you left the thimble men
   And came with me away;

For there again were thimble men
   And shooting galleries,
And card-trick men and Maggie men
   Of all sorts and degrees—
But not a sight of you, John-John,
              Was anywhere.

I turned my face to home again,
   And called myself a fool
To think you'd leave the thimble men
   And live again by rule,
And go to Mass and keep the fast
   And till the little patch:
My wish to have you home was past
   Before I raised the latch
And pushed the door and saw you, John,
              Sitting down there.

How cool you came in here, begad,
   As if you owned the place!
But rest yourself there now, my lad,
   'Tis good to see your face;
My dream is out, and now by it
   I think I know my mind:
At six o'clock this house you'll quit,
   And leave no grief behind;—
But until six o'clock, John-John,
             My bit you'll share

The neighbours' shame of me began
   When first I brought you in:
To wed and keep a tinker man
   They thought a kind of sin;

But now this three year since you're gone
    'Tis pity me they do,
And that I'd rather have, John-John,
    Than that they'd pity you.
Pity for me and you, John-John,
                    I could not bear.

Oh, you're my husband right enough,
    But what's the good of that?
You know you never were the stuff
    To be the cottage cat,
To watch the fire and hear me lock
    The door and put out Shep—
But there now, it is six o'clock
    And time for you to step.
God bless and keep you far, John-John!
                    And that's my prayer.

116   *Of a Poet Patriot*

HIS songs were a little phrase
    Of eternal song,
Drowned in the harping of lays
    More loud and long.

His deed was a single word,
    Called out alone
In a night when no echo stirred
    To laughter or moan.

But his songs new souls shall thrill,
    The loud harps dumb,
And his deed the echoes fill
    When the dawn is come.

163

117 *The Yellow Bittern*

(*From the Irish of Cathal Buidhe Mac Giolla Ghunna*)

THE yellow bittern that never broke out
  In a drinking bout, might as well have drunk;
His bones are thrown on a naked stone
  Where he lived alone like a hermit monk.
O yellow bittern! I pity your lot,
  Though they say that a sot like myself is curst—
I was sober a while, but I'll drink and be wise
  For I fear I should die in the end of thirst.

It's not for the common birds that I'd mourn,
  The black-bird, the corn-crake, or the crane,
But for the bittern that's shy and apart
  And drinks in the marsh from the lone bog-drain.
Oh! if I had known you were near your death,
  While my breath held out I'd have run to you,
Till a splash from the Lake of the Son of the Bird
  Your soul would have stirred and waked anew.

My darling told me to drink no more
  Or my life would be o'er in a little short while;
But I told her 'tis drink gives me health and strength
  And will lengthen my road by many a mile.
You see how the bird of the long smooth neck
  Could get his death from the thirst at last—
Come, son of my soul, and drain your cup,
  You'll get no sup when your life is past.

In a wintering island by Constantine's halls
  A bittern calls from a wineless place,
And tells me that hither he cannot come
  Till the summer is here and the sunny days.

When he crosses the stream there and wings o'er the sea
   Then a fear comes to me he may fail in his flight—
Well, the milk and the ale are drunk every drop,
   And a dram won't stop our thirst this night.

118   *The Night Hunt*

IN the morning, in the dark,
When the stars begin to blunt,
By the wall of Barna Park
Dogs I heard and saw them hunt.
All the parish dogs were there,
All the dogs for miles around,
Teeming up behind a hare,
In the dark, without a sound.

How I heard I scarce can tell—
'Twas a patter in the grass—
And I did not see them well
Come across the dark and pass;
Yet I saw them and I knew
Spearman's dog and Spellman's dog
And, beside my own dog too,
Leamy's from the Island Bog.

In the morning when the sun
Burnished all the green to gorse,
I went out to take a run
Round the bog upon my horse;
And my dog that had been sleeping
In the heat beside the door
Left his yawning and went leaping
On a hundred yards before.

THOMAS MacDONAGH

Through the village street we passed—
Not a dog there raised a snout—
Through the street and out at last
On the white bog road and out
Over Barna Park full pace,
Over to the Silver Stream,
Horse and dog in happy race,
Rider between thought and dream.

By the stream at Leamy's house,
Lay a dog—my pace I curbed—
But our coming did not rouse
Him from drowsing undisturbed;
And my dog, as unaware
Of the other, dropped beside
And went running by me there
With my horse's slackened stride.

Yet by something, by a twitch
Of the sleeper's eye, a look
From the runner, something which
Little chords of feeling shook,
I was conscious that a thought
Shuddered through the silent deep
Of a secret—I had caught
Something I had known in sleep.

LORD DUNSANY

1878–1957

The Memory

I WATCH the doctors walking with the nurses to and fro
And I hear them softly talking in the garden where they go,
But I envy not their learning, nor their right of walking
free,
For the emperor of Tartary has died for love of me.

I can see his face all golden beneath his night-black hair,
And the temples strange and olden in the gleaming eastern
air,
Where he walked alone and sighing because I would not
sail
To the lands where he was dying for a love of no avail.

He had seen my face by magic in a mirror that they make
For those rulers proud and tragic by their lotus-covered
lake,
Where there hangs a pale-blue tiling on an alabaster wall.
And he loved my way of smiling, and loved nothing else
at all.

There were peacocks there and peaches, and green monu-
ments of jade,
Where macaws with sudden screeches made the little dogs
afraid,
And the silver fountains sprinkled foreign flowers on the
sward
As they rose and curved and tinkled for their listless yellow
lord.

Ah well, he's dead and rotten in his far magnolia grove,
But his love is unforgotten and I need no other love,
And with open eyes when sleeping, or closed eyes when
    awake,
I can see the fountains leaping by the borders of the lake.

They call it my delusion; they may call it what they will,
For the times are in confusion and are growing wilder still,
And there are no splendid memories in any face I see.
But an emperor of Tartary has died for love of me.

120   *On the Safe Side*

I MET a man in older lands
    And nearer to the sun than these
Who tended with devoted hands
    An idol on his mantelpiece.

I asked him, 'Why the marigolds,
    And perfumed sticks you burn away,
And why the lily that he holds,
    When he is only painted clay?'

He answered, 'Lest it should be true
    What he who sold the idol said:
Long since this idol filled the blue
    With all the stars that he had made,

And not a moon and not a sun
    But he has rounded it with care
And set them floating one by one
    In all the spaces of the air.

And lest this should be true indeed
  And lest the idol one day tire
Of all the splendour and the speed
  Of stars that drift at his desire,

And lest he make a lovelier star
  Than any that the sky has known,
With gardens in it fairer far
  Than ours, when ours are overthrown,

And there, from dust when I am dead
  Creating me, again, set me;
With sweetest scents, I wash his head,
  With incense-sticks I give him glee,

With marigolds I make a glow
  About his presence day by day,
Although at Oxford long ago
  We held that he was only clay.'

OLIVER ST. JOHN GOGARTY

1878–1957

121   *Non Dolet*

OUR friends go with us as we go
Down the long path where Beauty wends,
Where all we love foregathers, so
Why should we fear to join our friends?

Who would survive them to outlast
His children; to outwear his fame—
Left when the Triumph has gone past—
To win from Age, not Time a name?

Then do not shudder at the knife
That Death's indifferent hand drives home;
But with the Strivers leave the Strife,
Nor, after Caesar, skulk in Rome.

122   *Golden Stockings*

GOLDEN stockings you had on
In the meadow where you ran;
And your little knees together
Bobbed like pippins in the weather,
When the breezes rush and fight
For those dimples of delight,
And they dance from the pursuit
And the leaf looks like the fruit.

I have many a sight in mind
That would last if I were blind;
Many verses I could write
That would bring me many a sight.
Now I only see but one,
See you running in the sun,
And the gold-dust coming up
From the trampled buttercup.

123   *Per Iter Tenebricosum*

ENOUGH! Why should a man bemoan
A Fate that leads the natural way?
Or think himself a worthier one
Than those who braved it in their day?
If only gladiators died,
Or Heroes, Death would be his pride;
But have not little maidens gone,
And Lesbia's sparrow—all alone?

The Crab Tree

HERE is the crab tree,
Firm and erect,
In spite of the thin soil,
In spite of neglect.
The twisted root grapples
For sap with the rock,
And draws the hard juice
To the succulent top:
Here are wild apples,
Here's a tart crop!

No outlandish grafting
That ever grew soft
In a sweet air of Persia,
Or safe Roman croft;
Unsheltered by steading,
Rock-rooted and grown,
A great tree of Erin,
It stands up alone,
A forest tree spreading
Where forests are gone.

Of all who pass by it
How few in it see
A westering remnant
Of days when Lough Neagh
Flowed up the long dingles
Its blossom had lit,
Old days of a glory
Time cannot repeat;
And therefore it mingles
The bitter and sweet.

171

It takes from the West Wind
The thrust of the main;
It makes from the tension
Of sky and of plain,
Of what clay enacted,
Of living alarm,
A vitalised symbol
Of earth and of storm,
Of Chaos contracted
To intricate form.

Unbreakable wrestler!
What sapling or herb
Has core of such sweetness
And fruit so acerb?
So grim a transmitter
Of life through mishap,
That one wonders whether
If that in the sap
Is sweet or is bitter
Which makes it stand up.

125   *To the Liffey with the Swans*

KEEP you these calm and lovely things,
    And float them on your clearest water;
For one would not disgrace a King's
    Transformed beloved and buoyant daughter.

And with her goes this sprightly swan,
    A bird of more than royal feather,
With alban beauty clothed upon:
    O keep them fair and well together!

As fair as was that doubled Bird,
  By love of Leda so besotten,
That she was all with wonder stirred,
  And the Twin Sportsmen were begotten!

SEUMAS O'SULLIVAN

1879–1958

126   *The Others*

FROM our hidden places
By a secret path,
We come in the moonlight
To the edge of the green rath.

There the night through
We take our pleasure,
Dancing to such a measure
As earth never knew.

To song and dance
And lilt without a name,
So sweetly breathed
'Twould put a bird to shame.

And many a young maiden
Is there, of mortal birth,
Her young eyes laden
With dreams of earth.

And many a youth entrancèd
Moves slowly in the wildered round,
His brave lost feet enchanted
In the rhythm of elfin sound.

173

Music so forest wild
And piercing sweet, would bring
Silence on blackbirds singing
Their best in the ear of Spring.

And now they pause in their dancing
And look with troubled eyes,
Earth's straying children
With sudden memory wise.

They pause, and their eyes in the moonlight
With faery wisdom cold,
Grow dim and a thought goes fluttering
In hearts no longer old.

And then the dream forsakes them
And sighing, they turn anew
As the whispering music takes them
To the dance of the elfin crew.

Oh, many a thrush and a blackbird
Would fall to the dewy ground
And pine away in silence
For envy of such a sound.

So the night through
In our sad pleasure,
We dance to many a measure
That earth never knew.

127   *Nelson Street*

THERE is hardly a mouthful of air
In the room where the breakfast is set,
For the blind is still down tho' it's late,
And the curtains are redolent yet

Of tobacco smoke, stale from last night.
There's the little bronze teapot, and there
The rashers and eggs on a plate,
And the sleepy canary, a hen,
Starts faintly her chirruping tweet,
And I know could she speak she would say:
'Hullo there—what's wrong with the light?
Draw the blind up, let's look at the day.'
I see that it's Monday again,
For the man with the organ is there;
Every Monday he comes to the street
(Lest I, or the bird there, should miss
Our count of monotonous days)
With his reed-organ, wheezy and sweet,
And stands by the window and plays
'There's a Land that is Fairer than This.'

128 ## The Land War

SORROW is over the fields,
The fields that never can know
The joy that the harvest yields
When the corn stands row on row.

But alien the cattle feed
Where many a furrow lies,
For the furrows remember the seed,
And the men have a dream in their eyes.

Not so did the strong men dream
E'er the fathers of these were born,
And the sons have remembered their deeds
As the fields have remembered the corn.

129

A Piper

A PIPER in the street today,
Set up, and tuned, and started to play,
And away, away, away on the tide
Of his music we started; on every side
Doors and windows were opened wide,
And men left down their work and came,
And women with petticoats coloured like flame,
And little bare feet that were blue with cold,
Went dancing back to the age of gold,
And all the world went gay, went gay,
For half an hour in the street today.

130

The Lamplighter

HERE to the leisured side of life,
Remote from traffic, free from strife,
A cul-de-sac, a sanctuary
Where old quaint customs creep to die
And only ancient memories stir,
At evening comes the lamplighter;
With measured steps, without a sound,
He treads the unalterable round,
Soundlessly touching one by one
The waiting posts that stand to take
The faint blue bubbles in his wake;
And when the night begins to wane
He comes to take them back again,
Before the chilly dawn can blight
The delicate frail buds of light.

131 ## Birds

TRULY these women are like birds; they take
Their pleasures delicately; now they stand
Upon the pavement with a foot upraised,
Nestling an ankled softness. Now launch out
Across the crowded street, scarce touching it,
Like water-hens across the sedgy lake,
Or stand in sunlight preening, like a bird
Above still water, or, when rain looms dark,
Crowd into some tall doorway wing by wing,
Like peacocks under yew trees in the Park,
Delicate and delightful and absurd,
Then venture forth again. Upgathering
Feather-like frills, they step demure as nuns,
Nor heed the menacing eyes on every side,
Dead set unceasingly like levelled guns,
Truly I think each woman is a bird.

132 ## The Sheep

SLOWLY they pass
In the grey of the evening
Over the wet road,
A flock of sheep.
Slowly they wend
In the grey of the gloaming
Over the wet road
That winds through the town.
Slowly they pass,
And gleaming whitely
Vanish away
In the grey of the evening.

Ah, what memories
Loom for a moment,
Gleam for a moment,
And vanish away,
Of the white days
When we two together
Went in the evening
Where the sheep lay,
We two together,
Went with slow feet
In the grey of the evening,
Where the sheep lay.
Whitely they gleam
For a moment, and vanish
Away in the dimness
Of sorrowful years,
Gleam for a moment,
All white, and go fading
Away in the greyness
Of sundering years.

PADRAIC PEARSE

1879–1916

133

The Wayfarer

THE beauty of the world hath made me sad,
This beauty that will pass;
Sometimes my heart hath shaken with great joy
To see a leaping squirrel in a tree,
Or a red lady-bird upon a stalk,
Or little rabbits in a field at evening,

Lit by a slanting sun,
Or some green hill where shadows drifted by,
Some quiet hill where mountainy man hath sown
And soon will reap, near to the gate of Heaven;
Or children with bare feet upon the sands
Of some ebbed sea, or playing on the streets
Of little towns in Connacht,
Things young and happy.
And then my heart hath told me:
These will pass,
Will pass and change, will die and be no more,
Things bright and green, things young and happy;
And I have gone upon my way
Sorrowful.

JOSEPH CAMPBELL

1879–1941

The Old Woman

134

As a white candle
In a holy place,
So is the beauty
Of an aged face.

As the spent radiance
Of the winter sun,
So is a woman
With her travail done.

Her brood gone from her,
And her thoughts as still
As the waters
Under a ruined mill.

135   *Blanaid's Song*

BLANAID loves roses;
And Lugh who disposes
All beautiful things,
Gave her
     Roses.

All heavenly things,
Dreambegot, fairyborn,
All natural things
Of colour and savour:
(Shawls of old kings,
Ripeness of corn,
Butterfly wings,
Veined chestnut leaves,
Dark summer eves,
Moons at high morn).
He searched for a favour,
And, pondering, gave her
     Roses.

Blanaid's black head
Wears a barret of red
From Lugh's gardenlands;
Her breasts and her hands
Are burthened with
     Roses.

—So her song closes!

136   *The Dancer*

THE tall dancer dances
With slowly taken breath:
In his feet music,
And on his face death.

His face is a mask,
It is so still and white:
His withered eyes shut,
Unmindful of light.

The old fiddler fiddles
The merry '*Silver Tip*'
With softly beating foot
And laughing eye and lip.

And round the dark walls
The people sit and stand,
Praising the art
Of the dancer of the land.

But he dances there
As if his kin were dead:
Clay in his thoughts,
And lightning in his tread!

137   *Chesspieces*

IT was a time of trouble—executions,
Dearth, searches, nightly firing, balked escapes—
And I sat silent, while my cellmate figured
Ruy Lopez' Gambit from the 'Praxis'. Silence

Best fitted with our mood: we seldom spoke.
'I have a thought,' he said, tilting his stool.
'We prisoners are so many pieces taken,
Swept from the board, only used again
When a new game is started.' 'There's that hope,'
I said, 'the hope of being used again.
Some day of strength, when ploughs are out in March,
The Dogs of Fionn will slip their iron chains,
And, heedless of torn wounds and failing wind,
Will run the old grey Wolf to death at last.'
He smiled, 'I like the image. My fat Kings
And painted Queens, and purple-cassocked Bishops
Are tame, indeed, beside your angry Dogs!'

ALICE MILLIGAN

1880–1953

138   *When I was a Little Girl*

WHEN I was a little girl,
In a garden playing
A thing was often said
To chide us delaying:

When after sunny hours,
At twilight's falling,
Down through the garden walks
Came our old nurse calling,

'Come in! for it's growing late,
And the grass will wet ye!
Come in! or when it's dark
The Fenians will get ye.'

Then, at this dreadful news,
All helter-skelter,
The panic-struck little flock
Ran home for shelter.

And round the nursery fire
Sat still to listen,
Fifty bare toes on the hearth,
Ten eyes a-glisten.

To hear of a night in March,
And loyal folk waiting,
To see a great army of men
Come devastating.

An Army of Papists grim,
With a green flag o'er them,
Red-coats and black police
Flying before them.

But God (Who our nurse declared
Guards British dominions)
Sent down a fall of snow
And scattered the Fenians.

'But somewhere they're lurking yet,
Maybe they're near us,'
Four little hearts pit-a-pat
Thought 'Can they hear us?'

Then the wind-shaken pane
Sounded like drumming;
'Oh!' they cried, 'tuck us in,
The Fenians are coming!'

Four little pairs of hands
In the cots where she led those,
Over their frightened heads
Pulled up the bedclothes.

But one little rebel there,
Watching all with laughter,
Thought, 'When the Fenians come
I'll rise and go after.'

Wished she had been a boy
And a good deal older—
Able to walk for miles
With a gun on her shoulder.

Able to lift aloft
The Green Flag o'er them
(Red-coats and black police
Flying before them).

And, as she dropped asleep,
Was wondering whether
God, if they prayed to Him,
Would give fine weather.

BLANAID SALKELD

1880–

139   *Anchises*

I WISH he were the Polar Star in Heaven,
Or the little Pleiads seven,

184

And I would be the best astronomer
That ever watched for even.
I wish he were the Sun from East to West—
Even for me to see . . . What of the rest?—
I would not grudge their share, or mind . . .
Or if he were the Wind,
Then he would seek out sometimes me, even me.
Or if he were a bird of any kind,
I'd have his cry so fair,
I'd lure him into any snare—
And then, would I not free him?—
But since nowhere I see him,
Sometimes, in my sad breast,
I wish him dead, best.

140   *Youth*

THIS brief common youth I was once in dread for it
That fled like a thief off with goods not paid for
Yet I am no poorer that saw all flit
To be one's own there is much to be said for it
O it's many the good deed I delayed for it
Thinking youth's merchandise worthy to trade for
A fugitive thief without grace or wit
Alas for the many have been struck dead for it
I turned from learning though I had the head for it
Dreaming youth's tone had the music I prayed for
But the strings snapped and the tunes were unwrit
Not to be bought back the wealth I betrayed for it.

That Corner

MAN is most anxious not to stir
Out of the unblessed beat
Of sounds that recur
In house or on street.
Not only the birds' morning prayers,
But light steppings up stairs,
Rap on the bedroom door,
We have heart-beats for.
The postman's knock, though it spill
Rejection and vulgar bill—
At noon, the baker's basket creaks;
Hooves, hoots, factory-shrieks;
Hollow tattle of the trams;
Or a door slams;
Buzz of flies; chapel bells,
And a thousand sounds else.
The casual spirit poises,
Elegantly,
Tired of being free,
Between the usual noises.
Love's mood, however,
Is contrary to this hankering,
This holding on to the seat
Of life's speeding jolty car.
Love is in a fever
To escape the tinkering
Minutes that beat—
Familiar,
Only varied by fear—
On eye and ear.
Now I would leap clear.

What bait shall I procure to lure him out of time?
Not from the sea into the salty drought—
But cleanly out
Of days' and nights' faint metre and false rhyme,
To hold him safe
Round final angle,
Corner, where no jangle-tangle
Makes stir to chafe:
From this inadequate night and day,
I would steal him away.

ROBIN FLOWER

1881–1946

(*Translations from the Irish*)

142   *Pangur Bán*

I and Pangur Bán, my cat,
'Tis a like task we are at;
Hunting mice is his delight,
Hunting words I sit all night.

Better far than praise of men
'Tis to sit with book and pen;
Pangur bears me no ill will,
He too plies his simple skill.

'Tis a merry thing to see
At our tasks how glad are we,
When at home we sit and find
Entertainment to our mind.

Oftentimes a mouse will stray
In the hero Pangur's way;
Oftentimes my keen thought set
Takes a meaning in its net.

'Gainst the wall he sets his eye
Full and fierce and sharp and sly;
'Gainst the wall of knowledge I
All my little wisdom try.

When a mouse darts from its den,
O how glad is Pangur then!
O what gladness do I prove
When I solve the doubts I love!

So in peace our tasks we ply,
Pangur Bán, my cat and I;
In our hearts we find our bliss,
I have mine and he has his.

Practice every day has made
Pangur perfect in his trade;
I get wisdom day and night
Turning darkness into light.

143   *The Dispraise of Absalom*

VEILED in that light amazing,
Lady, your hair soft-wavèd
Has cast into dispraising
Absalom son of David.

Your golden locks close clinging,
Like birdflocks of strange seeming,
Silent with no sweet singing
Draw all men into dreaming.

That bright hair idly flowing
Over the keen eyes' brightness,
Like gold rings set with glowing
Jewels of crystal lightness.

Strange loveliness that lingers
From lands that hear the Siren:
No ring enclasps your fingers,
Gold rings your neck environ,

Gold chains of hair that cluster
Round the neck straight and slender,
Which to that shining muster
Yields in a sweet surrender.

144 *At Mass*

AH! light lovely lady with delicate lips aglow,
With breast more white than a branch heavy-laden with
        snow,
When my hand was uplifted at Mass to salute the Host
I looked at you once, and the half of my soul was lost.

145 *He Praises His Wife when She had*
Gone from Him

WHITE hands of languorous grace,
Fair feet of stately pace
And snowy-shining knees—
My love was made of these.

Stars glimmered in her hair,
Slim was she, satin-fair;
Dark like seal's fur her brows
Shadowed her cheek's fresh rose.

What words can match its worth,
That beauty closed in earth,
That courteous, stately air
Winsome and shy and fair.

To have known all this and be
Tortured with memory
—Curse on this waking breath—
Makes me in love with death.

Better to sleep than see
This house now dark to me
A lonely shell in place
Of that unrivalled grace.

JAMES JOYCE
1882–1941

146   *Tutto è Sciolto*

A BIRDLESS heaven, seadusk, one lone star
Piercing the west,
As thou, fond heart, love's time, so faint, so far,
Rememberest.

The clear young eyes' soft look, the candid brow,
The fragrant hair,
Falling as through the silence falleth now
Dusk of the air.

Why then, remembering those shy
Sweet lures, repine
When the dear love she yielded with a sigh
Was all but thine?

147 *I Hear an Army*

I HEAR an army charging upon the land,
  And the thunder of horses plunging, foam about their
    knees:
Arrogant, in black armour, behind them stand,
  Disdaining the reins, with fluttering whips, the
    charioteers.

They cry unto the night their battle name:
  I moan in sleep when I hear afar their whirling laughter.
They cleave the gloom of dreams, a blinding flame,
  Clanging, clanging upon the heart as upon an anvil.

They come shaking in triumph their long, green hair:
  They come out of the sea and run shouting by the shore.
My heart, have you no wisdom thus to despair?
  My love, my love, my love, why have you left me alone?

148 *What Counsel has the Hooded Moon*

WHAT counsel has the hooded moon
  Put in thy heart, my shyly sweet,
Of Love in ancient plenilune,
  Glory and stars beneath his feet—
A sage that is but kith and kin
With the comedian Capuchin?

191

Believe me rather that am wise
   In disregard of the divine,
A glory kindles in those eyes
   Trembles to starlight. Mine, O Mine!
No more be tears in moon or mist
For thee, sweet sentimentalist.

149 From Molly Bloom's Soliloquy—*Ulysses*

HE said I was a flower of the mountain yes so we are flowers
all a womans body yes that was one true thing he said in his
life and the sun shines for you today yes that was why I
liked him because I saw he understood or felt what a woman
is and I knew I could always get round him and I gave him
all the pleasure I could leading him on till he asked me to
say yes and I wouldnt answer first only looked out over the
sea and the sky I was thinking of so many things he didnt
know of Mulvey and Mr Stanhope and Hester and father
and old captain Groves and the sailors playing all birds fly
and I say stoop and washing up dishes they called it on the
pier and the sentry in front of the governors house with the
thing round his white helmet poor devil half roasted and
the Spanish girls laughing in their shawls and their tall
combs and the auctions in the morning the Greeks and the
Jews and the Arabs and the devil knows who else from all
the ends of Europe and Duke street and the fowl market
all clucking outside Larby Sharons and the poor donkeys
slipping half asleep and the vague fellows in the cloaks
asleep in the shade on the steps and the big wheels of the
carts of the bulls and the old castle thousands of years old
yes and those handsome Moors all in white and turbans
like kings asking you to sit down in their little bit of a shop

and Ronda with the old windows of the posadas glancing
eyes a lattice hid for her lover to kiss the iron and the wine
shops half open at night and the castanets and the night we
missed the boat at Algeciras the watchman going about
serene with his lamp and O that awful deep down torrent
O and the sea the sea crimson sometimes like fire and the
glorious sunsets and the figtrees in the Alameda gardens
yes and all the queer little streets and pink and blue and
yellow houses and the rose gardens and the jessamine and
geraniums and cactuses and Gibraltar as a girl where I was
a Flower of the mountain yes when I put the rose in my
hair like the Andalusian girls used or shall I wear a red yes
and how he kissed me under the Moorish wall and I thought
well as well him as another and then I asked him with my
eyes to ask again yes and then he asked me would I yes
to say yes my mountain flower and first I put my arms
around him yes and drew him down to me so he could feel
my breasts all perfume yes and his heart was going like mad
and yes I said yes I will Yes.

150   From *Finnegans Wake*

Nuvoletta

THEN Nuvoletta reflected for the last time in her little long
life and she made up all her myriads of drifting minds in
one. She cancelled all her engauzements. She climbed over
the bannistars; she gave a childy cloudy cry: *Nuée! Nuée!*
A lightdress fluttered. She was gone. And into the river that
had been a stream (for a thousand of tears had gone eon her
and come on her and she was stout and struck on dancing
and her muddied name was Missisliffi) there fell a tear, a
singult tear, the loveliest of all tears . . . for it was a leaptear.

But the river tripped on her by and by, lapping as though her heart was brook: *Why, why, why! Weh, O weh! I'se so silly to be flowing but I no canna stay!*

Anna Livia Plurabelle

AND after that she wove a garland for her hair. She pleated it. She plaited it. Of meadowgrass and riverflags, the bulrush and waterweed, and of fallen griefs of weeping willow. Then she made her bracelets and her anklets and her armlets and a jetty amulet for necklace of clicking cobbles and pattering pebbles and rumbledown rubble, richmond and rehr, of Irish rhunerhinerstones and shellmarble bangles. That done, a dawk of smut to her airy ey, Annushka Lutetiavitch Pufflovah, and the lellipos cream to her lippeleens and the pick of the paintbox for her pommettes, from strawbirry reds to extra violates.

The End or the Beginning

I'M passing out. O bitter ending! I'll slip away before they're up. They'll never see. Nor know. Nor miss me. And it's old and old it's sad and old it's sad and weary I go back to you, my cold father, my cold mad father, my cold mad feary father, till the near sight of the mere size of him, the moyles and moyles of it, moananoaning, makes me seasilt saltsick and I rush, my only, into your arms. I see them rising! Save me from those therrble prongs! Two more. Onetwo moremens more. So. Avelaval. My leaves have drifted from me. All. But one clings still. I'll bear it on me. To remind me of. Lff! So soft this morning, ours. Yes. Carry me along, taddy, like you done through the toy fair! If I seen him bearing down on me now under whitespread wings like he'd come from Arkangels, I sink I'd die

194

down over his feet, humbly dumbly, only to washup. Yes,
tid. There's where. First. We pass through grass behush
the bush to. Whish! A gull. Gulls. Far calls. Coming, far!
End here. Us then. Finn, again! Take. Bussoftlhee, meme-
mormee! Till thousendsthee. Lps. The keys to. Given!
A way a lone a last a loved a long the

PADRAIC COLUM

1882–

151   *An Old Man Said*

AN old man said, 'I saw
The chief of the things that are gone;
A stag with head held high,
A doe, and a fawn;

'And they were the deer of Ireland
That scorned to breed within bound:
The last; they left no race
Tame on a pleasure-ground.

'A stag, with his hide all rough
With the dew, and a doe and a fawn;
Nearby, on their track on the mountain,
I watched them, two and one,

'Down to the Shannon going—
Did its waters cease to flow,
When they passed, they that carried the swiftness,
And the pride of long ago?

'The last of the troop that had heard
Finn's and Oscar's cry;
A doe and a fawn, and before
A stag with head held high!'

152   *A Drover*

To Meath of the pastures,
From wet hills by the sea,
Through Leitrim and Longford,
Go my cattle and me.

I hear in the darkness
Their slipping and breathing—
I name them the by-ways
They're to pass without heeding;

Then the wet, winding roads,
Brown bogs with black water,
And my thoughts on white ships
And the King o' Spain's daughter.

O farmer, strong farmer!
You can spend at the fair,
But your face you must turn
To your crops and your care;

And soldiers, red soldiers!
You've seen many lands,
But you walk two by two,
And by captain's commands!

O the smell of the beasts,
The wet wind in the morn,
And the proud and hard earth
Never broken for corn!

And the crowds at the fair,
The herds loosened and blind,
Loud words and dark faces,
And the wild blood behind!

(O strong men with your best
I would strive breast to breast,
I could quiet your herds,
With my words, with my words!)

I will bring you, my kine,
Where there's grass to the knee,
But you'll think of scant croppings
Harsh with salt of the sea.

153   *A Cradle Song*

O, MEN from the fields!
Come gently within.
Tread softly, softly,
O! men coming in.

Mavourneen is going
From me and from you,
Where Mary will fold him
With mantle of blue!

197

From reek of the smoke
And cold of the floor,
And the peering of things
Across the half-door.

O, men from the fields!
Soft, softly come thro'.
Mary puts round him
Her mantle of blue.

154   *A Poor Scholar of the Forties*

MY eyelids red and heavy are,
With bending o'er the smould'ring peat.
I know the Aeneid now by heart,
My Virgil read in cold and heat,
In loneliness and hunger smart.
    And I know Homer, too, I ween,
    As Munster poets know Ossian.

And I must walk this road that winds
'Twixt bog and bog, while east there lies
A city with its men and books,
With treasures open to the wise,
Heart-words from equals, comrade-looks;
    Down here they have but tale and song
    They talk Repeal the whole night long.

'You teach Greek verbs and Latin nouns,'
The dreamer of Young Ireland said.
'You do not hear the muffled call,
The sword being forged, the far-off tread
Of hosts to meet as Gael and Gall—
    What good to us your wisdom store,
    Your Latin verse, your Grecian lore?'

And what to me is Gael or Gall?
Less than the Latin or the Greek.
I teach these by the dim rush-light,
In smoky cabins night and week.
But what avail my teaching slight?
   Years hence, in rustic speech a phrase,
   As in wild earth a Grecian vase!

155   *The Burial of Saint Brendan*

ON the third day from this (Saint Brendan said)
I will be where no wind that filled a sail
Has ever been, and it blew high or low:
For from this home-creek, from this body's close
I shall put forth: make ready, you, to go
With what remains to Cluan Hy-many,
For there my resurrection I'd have be.

But you will know how hard they'll strive to hold
This body o' me, and hold it for the place
Where I was bred, they say, and born and reared.
For they would have my resurrection here,
So that my sanctity might be matter shared
By every mother's child the tribeland polled
Who lived and died and mixed into the mould.

So you will have to use all canniness
To bring this body to its burial
When in your hands I leave what goes in clay;
The wagon that our goods are carried in—
Have it yoked up between the night and day,
And when the breath is from my body gone,
Bear body out, the wagon lay it on;

And cover it with gear that's taken hence—
'The goods of Brendan is what's here,' you'll say
To those who'll halt you; they will pass you then:
Tinkers and tailors, soldiers, farmers, smiths,
You'll leave beside their doors—all those thwart men
For whom my virtue was a legacy
That they would profit in, each a degree—

As though it were indeed some chalice, staff,
Crozier or casket, that they might come to,
And show to those who chanced upon the way,
And have, not knowing how the work was done
In scrolls and figures and in bright inlay:
Whence came the gold and silver that they prize,
The blue enamels and the turquoises!

I, Brendan, had a name came from the sea—
I was the first who sailed the outer main,
And past all forelands and all fastnesses!
I passed the voiceless anchorites, their isles,
Saw the ice-palaces upon the seas,
Mentioned Christ's name to men cut off from men,
Heard the whales snort, and saw the Kraken!

And on a wide-branched, green and glistening tree
Beheld the birds that had been angels erst:
Between the earth and heaven 'twas theirs to wing:
Fallen from High they were, but they had still
Music of Heaven's Court: I heard them sing:
Even now that island of the unbeached coast
I see, and hear the white, resplendent host!

For this they'd have my burial in this place,
Their hillside, and my resurrection be

Out of the mould that they with me would share.
But I have chosen Cluan for my ground—
A happy place! Some grace came to me there:
And you, as you go towards it, to men say,
Should any ask you on that long highway:

'Brendan is here, who had great saints for friends:
Ita, who reared him on a mother's knee,
Enda, who from his fastness blessed his sail:
Then Brighid, she who had the flaming heart,
And Colum-cille, prime of all the Gael;
Gildas of Britain, wisest child of light.'
And saying this, drive through the falling night.

JAMES STEPHENS

1882–1950

156   *O Bruadair*

(*From the Irish of O Bruadair*)

I WILL sing no more songs: the pride of my country I sang
Through forty long years of good rhyme, without any
    avail;
And no one cared even as much as the half of a hang
For the song or the singer, so here is the end to the tale.

If a person should think I complain and have not got the
    cause,
Let him bring his eyes here and take a good look at my hand,
Let him say if a goose-quill has calloused this poor pair of
    paws
Or the spade that I grip on and dig with out there in the
    land?

When the great ones were safe and renowned and were
    rooted and tough,
Though my mind went to them and took joy in the for-
    tune of those,
And pride in their pride and their fame, they gave little
    enough,
Not as much as two boots for my feet, or an old suit of
    clothes.

I ask of the Craftsman that fashioned the fly and the bird,
Of the Champion whose passion will lift me from death in
    a time,
Of the Spirit that melts icy hearts with the wind of a word,
That my people be worthy, and get better singing than mine.

I had hoped to live decent, when Ireland was quit of her care,
As a bailiff or steward perhaps in a house of degree,
But the end of the tale is, old brogues and old britches to
    wear,
So I'll sing no more songs for the men that care nothing
    for me.

157   *The Goat Paths*

    THE crooked paths go every way
        Upon the hill—they wind about
        Through the heather in and out
    Of the quiet sunniness.
    And there the goats, day after day,
        Stray in sunny quietness,
    Cropping here and cropping there,
        As they pause and turn and pass,
    Now a bit of heather spray,
        Now a mouthful of the grass.

In the deeper sunniness,
    In the place where nothing stirs,
Quietly in quietness,
    In the quiet of the furze,
For a time they come and lie
Staring on the roving sky.
If you approach they run away,
    They leap and stare, away they bound,
    With a sudden angry sound,
To the sunny quietude;
    Crouching down where nothing stirs
    In the silence of the furze,
Crouching down again to brood
    In the sunny solitude.

If I were as wise as they
    I would stray apart and brood,
I would beat a hidden way
Through the quiet heather spray
    To a sunny solitude;
And should you come I'd run away,
    I would make an angry sound,
    I would stare and turn and bound
To the deeper quietude,
    To the place where nothing stirs
    In the silence of the furze.
In that airy quietness
    I would think as long as they;
Through the quiet sunniness
    I would stray away to brood
By a hidden beaten way
    In a sunny solitude.

I would think until I found
    Something I can never find,
Something lying on the ground,
    In the bottom of my mind.

158   *The Snare*

I HEAR a sudden cry of pain!
    There is a rabbit in a snare:
Now I hear the cry again,
    But I cannot tell from where.

But I cannot tell from where
    He is calling out for aid;
Crying on the frightened air,
    Making everything afraid,

Making everything afraid
    Wrinkling up his little face,
As he cries again for aid;
    And I cannot find the place!

And I cannot find the place
    Where his paw is in the snare;
Little one! Oh, little one!
    I am searching everywhere.

159   *Blue Blood*
             (*From the Irish*)

WE thought at first, this man is a king for sure,
Or the branch of a mighty and ancient and famous lineage—
That silly, sulky, illiterate, blackavised boor
Who was hatched by foreign vulgarity under a hedge.

The good men of Clare were drinking his health in a flood,
And gazing with me in awe at the princely lad;
And asking each other from what bluest blueness of blood
His daddy was squeezed, and the pa of the da of his dad?

We waited there, gaping and wondering, anxiously,
Until he'd stop eating and let the glad tidings out,
And the slack-jawed booby proved to the hilt that he
Was lout, son of lout, by old lout, and was da to a lout!

'DERMOT O'BYRNE' (ARNOLD BAX)

1883–1953

160   *A Dublin Ballad—1916*

O WRITE it up above your hearth
And troll it out to sun and moon,
To all true Irishmen on earth
Arrest and death come late or soon.

Some boy-o whistled *Ninety-eight*
One Sunday night in College Green,
And such a broth of love and hate
Was stirred ere Monday morn was late
As Dublin town had never seen.

And god-like forces shocked and shook
Through Irish hearts that lively day,
And hope it seemed no ill could brook.
Christ! for that liberty they took
There was the ancient deuce to pay!

'DERMOT O'BYRNE'

The deuce in all his bravery,
His girth and gall grown no whit less,
He swarmed in from the fatal sea
With pomp of huge artillery
And brass and copper haughtiness.

He cracked up all the town with guns
That roared loud psalms to fire and death,
And houses hailed down granite tons
To smash our wounded underneath.

And when at last the golden bell
Of liberty was silenced—then
He learned to shoot extremely well
At unarmed Irish gentlemen!

Ah! where were Michael and gold Moll
And Seumas and my drowsy self?
Why did fate blot us from the scroll?
Why were we left upon the shelf,

Fooling with trifles in the dark
When the light struck so wild and hard?
Sure our hearts were as good a mark
For Tommies up before the lark
At rifle practice in the yard!

Well, the last fire is trodden down,
Our dead are rotting fast in lime,
We all can sneak back into town,
Stravague about as in old time,

And stare at gaps of grey and blue
Where Lower Mount Street used to be,
And where flies hum round muck we knew
For Abbey Street and Eden Quay.

And when the devil's made us wise
Each in his own peculiar hell,
With desert hearts and drunken eyes
We're free to sentimentalize
By corners where the martyrs fell.

FRANCIS MacNAMARA

1884–1946

161   *Diminutivus Ululans*

WAILING diminutive of me, be still;
   Or cry, but spare me that regretful tone,—
Of sorrows elemental waxing shrill,
   O you of living things the most alone!
   Son, do you thus reproach me and make moan,
Because upon Love's chariot I did fly
   And a horn winded in the great unknown,
Calling your atoms out to be an I?
Should I have let you in abeyance lie,
   Disintegrate another million years?
Then use your life to teach you how to die
   And pass again beyond the reach of tears,
Some day you may regret I dragged you thence,
Perhaps forgive the vast impertinence.

JOSEPH PLUNKETT

1887–1916

162   *I See His Blood upon the Rose*

I SEE his blood upon the rose
And in the stars the glory of his eyes,
His body gleams amid eternal snows,
His tears fall from the skies.

I see his face in every flower;
The thunder and the singing of the birds
Are but his voice—and carven by his power
Rocks are his written words.

All pathways by his feet are worn,
His strong heart stirs the ever-beating sea,
His crown of thorns is twined with every thorn,
His cross is every tree.

163   *The Claim that has the Canker on*
the Rose

THE claim that has the canker on the rose
Is mine on you, man's claim on Paradise
Hopelessly lost that ceaselessly he sighs
And all unmerited God still bestows;
The claim on the invisible wind that blows
The flame of charity to enemies
Not to the deadliest sinners, God denies—
Less claim than this have I on you, God knows.

I cannot ask for any thing from you
Because my pride is eaten up with shame
That you should think my poverty a claim
Upon your charity, knowing it is true
That all the glories formerly I knew
Shone from the cloudy splendour of your name.

164   *My Lady has the Grace of Death*

My lady has the grace of Death
Whose charity is quick to save,
Her heart is broad as heaven's breath,
Deep as the grave.

She found me fainting by the way
And fed me from her babeless breast
Then played with me as children play,
Rocked me to rest.

When soon I rose and cried to heaven
Moaning for sins I could not weep
She told me of her sorrows seven
Kissed me to sleep.

And when the morn rose bright and ruddy
And sweet birds sang on the branch above
She took my sword from her side all bloody
And died for love.

PATRICK BROWNE

1889–

165   *The Green Autumn Stubble*

(From the Irish)

WHEN stubble-lands were greening, you came among the
      stooks,
And grace was in your feet then, and love was in your looks,
In your cheeks the rose grew redder, and your hair in
      clusters lay,
And I would we lived together, or together slipped away.

I had a dream on Wednesday that bitter was the frost,
And I saw my love lamenting at dawn that I was lost;
Methought I came beside her and held her tenderly,
And all Erin I defied then to part my love and me.

My curse on him is spoken who keeps my love from me,
And swears that to our courting he never will agree;
For though skies should send the deluge or the snowy
      North its flakes,
We two could live as pleasant as the swans upon the lakes.

The sea-gull's heart is merry when the fish is in his beak,
And the eel within Lough Eyrne can swim from creek to
      creek,
And I spoke tripping Gaelic, and merry songs I've sung,
But now my wits are crazy and leaden is my tongue.

HELEN WADDELL
1889–

166   *The Day of Wrath*

(*From the Latin of St. Columba*)

D A Y of the king most righteous,
   The day is nigh at hand,
The day of wrath and vengeance,
   And darkness on the land.

Day of thick clouds and voices,
   Of mighty thundering,
A day of narrow anguish
   And bitter sorrowing.

The love of women's over,
   And ended is desire,
Men's strife with men is quiet
   And the world lusts no more.

BRINSLEY MacNAMARA
1890–

167   *On Seeing Swift in Laracor*

I S A W them walk that lane again
   And watch the midges cloud a pool,
Laughing at something in the brain—
   The Dean and Patrick Brell, the fool.

Like Lear he kept his fool with him
   Long into Dublin's afterglow,
Until the wits in him grew dim
   And Patrick sold him for a show.

Here were the days before Night came,
   When Stella and the other—'slut',
Vanessa, called by him—that flame
   When Laracor was Lilliput!

And here, by walking up and down,
   He made a man called Gulliver,
While bits of lads came out from town
   To have a squint at him and her.

Still, was it Stella that they saw,
   Or else some lassie of their own?
For in his story that's the flaw,
   The secret no one since has known.

Was it some wench among the corn
   Had set him from the other two,
Some tenderness that he had torn,
   Some lovely blossom that he knew?

For when Vanessa died of love,
   And Stella learned to keep her place,
His Dublin soon the story wove
   That steeped them in the Dean's disgrace.

They did not know, 'twas he could tell!
   The reason of his wildest rages,
The story kept by Patrick Brell,
   The thing that put him with the ages.

Now when they mention of the Dean
   Some silence holds them as they talk;
Some things there are unsaid, unseen,
   That drive me to this lonely walk,

To meet the mighty man again,
    And yet no comfort comes to me.
Although sometimes I see him plain,
    That silence holds the Hill of Bree.

For, though I think I'd know her well,
    I've never seen her on his arm,
Laughing with him, nor heard her tell
    She had forgiven all the harm.

And yet I'd like to know 'twere true,
    That here at last in Laracor,
Here in the memory of a few,
    There was this rest for him and her.

GEOFFREY TAYLOR

1890–1956

168   *Country Walk*

W E, not content with naming distant views,
Set out for, say, Croagh Patrick, Knock na Rea,
Or other celebrated mountain blue
Through not too great an intervening seen;
Losing by laneway, field or woodland path
Sight of our goal, but finding other sights
Of flower or fly or bird upon a bough;
Until the mountain-foot was reached—and then
What was there more but fly or flower or bird
And not the mountain we had seen from far?
So there the question was: Are flower and fly
And woodland way and country lane an end,

Or does the mountain's self become a means
Involving sweaty climbing? Paraphrase
Of Truth one seeks for, finding only truths;
And then not Truth as seen—but as seen from.

169 *Song*

ROUSING to rein his pad's head back
    And turning his own to stare
Up along Kentish downland track
    Spider-bright in the April air,
Oh! said the Pilgrim Chaucer,
    O, copper-coin her hair.

With Wop his dog in a Warwick lane
    And never a sonnet's sigh or care
Till, lifting an eye from the ripening grain,
    And all his wits at once aware,
Oh! said the Stratford Country Squire.
    O, carrots for her hair.

Way back early from Hampton Court,
    Less than normally here or there,
Fumbling after the right retort—
    Epigram, epitaph, into prayer—
Oh! said my Lord of Rochester,
    O, for her Titian hair.

Well, after these—and one may suppose
    Well after these and some to spare—
All with differently qualified oh's,
    A different view of a fair affair,
O who were you in a bus to say
    Oh! for her bonny red hair.

Nor, under and under not her hat
   The rarely covered or rarer bare,
By proof not flame-proof, this with that
   Who are you yet who dare compare?
Oh! coppery, carroty, Titian O,
   Her rust-red autumn-beech-leaf hair.

FRANCIS LEDWIDGE

1891–1917

170   *A Twilight in Middle March*

WITHIN the oak a throb of pigeon wings
Fell silent, and grey twilight hushed the fold,
And spiders' hammocks swung on half-oped things
That shook like foreigners upon our cold.
A gipsy lit a fire and made a sound
Of moving tins, and from an oblong moon
The river seemed to gush across the ground
To the cracked metre of a marching tune.

And then three syllables of melody
Dropped from a blackbird's flute, and died apart
Far in the dewy dark. No more but three,
Yet sweeter music never touched a heart
Neath the blue domes of London. Flute and reed
Suggesting feelings of the solitude
When will was all the Delphi I would heed,
Lost like a wind within a summer wood
From little knowledge where great sorrows brood.

171 *August*

SHE'LL come at dusky first of day,
White over yellow harvest's song.
Upon her dewy rainbow way
She shall be beautiful and strong.
The lidless eye of noon shall spray
Tan on her ankles in the hay,
Shall kiss her brown the whole day long.

I'll know her in the windrows, tall
Above the crickets of the hay.
I'll know her when her odd eyes fall,
One May-blue, one November-grey.
I'll watch her from the red barn wall
Take down her rusty scythe, and call,
And I will follow her away.

172 *Thomas MacDonagh*

HE shall not hear the bittern cry
In the wild sky, where he is lain,
Nor voices of the sweeter birds
Above the wailing of the rain.

Nor shall he know when loud March blows
Through slanting snows her fanfare shrill,
Blowing to flame the golden cup
Of many an upset daffodil.

But when the Dark Cow leaves the moor,
And pastures poor with greedy weeds,
Perhaps he'll hear her low at morn
Lifting her horn in pleasant meads.

173   *Lament for the Poets: 1916*

I HEARD the Poor Old Woman say:
'At break of day the fowler came,
And took my blackbirds from their songs
Who loved me well thro' shame and blame.

'No more from lovely distances
Their songs shall bless me mile by mile
Nor to white Ashbourne call me down
To wear my crown another while.

'With bended flowers the angels mark
For the skylark the place they lie,
From there its little family
Shall dip their wings first in the sky.

'And when the first surprise of flight
Sweet songs excite, from the far dawn
Shall there come blackbirds loud with love,
Sweet echoes of the singers gone.

'But in the lonely hush of eve
Weeping I grieve the silent bills.'
I heard the Poor Old Woman say
In Derry of the little hills.

174   *The Herons*

As I was climbing Ardán Mór
From the shore of Sheelin lake
I met the herons coming down
Before the water's wake.

And they were talking in their flight
Of dreamy ways the herons go
When all the hills are withered up
Nor any waters flow.

MARY DAVENPORT O'NEILL

1893–

175 *Galway*

I KNOW a town tormented by the sea,
And there time goes slow
That the people see it flow
And watch it drowsily,
And growing older hour by hour they say,
'Please God, to-morrow!
Then we will work and play,'
And their tall houses crumble away.
This town is eaten through with memory
Of pride and thick red Spanish wine and gold
And a great come and go;
But the sea is cold,
And the spare, black trees
Crouch in the withering breeze
That blows from the sea,
And the land stands bare and alone,
For its warmth is turned away
And its strength held in hard cold grey-blue stone;
And the people are heard to say,
Through the raving of the jealous sea,
'Please God, to-morrow!
Then we will work and play.'

THOMAS McGREEVY

1893–

Aodh Ruadh O Domhnaill

To STIEFÁN MACENNA

Juan de Juni the priest said,
Each J becoming H;

Berruguete, he said,
And the G was aspirate;

Ximenez, he said then
And aspirated first and last.

But he never said
And—it seemed odd—he
Never had heard
The aspirated name
Of the centuries-dead
Bright-haired young man
Whose grave I sought.

All day I passed
In greatly built gloom
From dusty gilt tomb
Marvellously wrought
To tomb
 Rubbing
At mouldy inscriptions
With fingers wetted with spit
And asking
Where I might find it
And failing

Yet when
Unhurried—
   Not as at home
   Where heroes, hanged, are buried
   With non-commissioned officers' bored maledictions
   Quickly in the gaol yard—

They brought
His blackening body
Here
To rest
Princes came
Walking
Behind it
And all Valladolid knew
And out to Simancas all knew
Where they buried Red Hugh.

ROBERT GRAVES

1895–

177   *Lust in Song*

THEIR cheeks are blotched for shame, their running verse
Stumbles, with marrow-bones the drunken diners
Pelt them as they delay:
It is a something fearful in the song
Plagues them, an unknown grief that like a churl
Goes commonplace in cowskin
And bursts unheralded, crowing and coughing,
An unpilled holly-club twirled in his hand,

Into their many-shielded, samite-curtained
Jewel-bright hall where twelve kings sit at chess
Over the white-bronze pieces and the gold,
And by a gross enchantment
Flails down the rafters and leads off the queens—
The wild-swan-breasted, the rose-ruddy-cheeked
Raven-haired daughters of their admiration—
To stir his black pots and to bed on straw.

178 *The Haunted House*

'COME, surly fellow, come! A song!'
  What, fools? sing to you?
Choose from the clouded tales of wrong
  And terror I bring to you:

Of a night so torn with cries,
  Honest men sleeping
Start awake with rabid eyes,
  Bone-chilled, flesh creeping,

Of spirits in the web-hung room
  Up above the stable,
Groans, knockings in the gloom,
  The dancing table,

Of demons in the dry well
  That cheep and mutter,
Clanging of an unseen bell,
  Blood choking the gutter,

Of lust filthy past belief
  Lurking unforgotten,
Unrestrainable endless grief
  In breasts long rotten.

221

A song? What laughter or what song
  Can this house remember?
Do flowers and butterflies belong
  To a blind December?

179   *In the Wilderness*

HE, of his gentleness,
Thirsting and hungering
Walked in the wilderness;
Soft words of grace he spoke
Unto lost desert-folk
That listened wondering.
He heard the bittern call
From ruined palace-wall,
Answered him brotherly;
He held communion
With the she-pelican
Of lonely piety.
Basilisk, cockatrice,
Flocked to his homilies,
With mail of dread device,
With monstrous barbed stings,
With eager dragon-eyes;
Great bats on leathern wings
And old, blind, broken things
Mean in their miseries.
Then ever with him went,
Of all his wanderings
Comrade, with ragged coat,
Gaunt ribs—poor innocent—
Bleeding foot, burning throat,
The guileless young scapegoat:

222

For forty nights and days
Followed in Jesus' ways,
Sure guard behind him kept,
Tears like a lover wept.

180 ## *Love Without Hope*

LOVE without hope, as when the young bird-catcher
Swept off his tall hat to the Squire's own daughter,
So let the imprisoned larks escape and fly
Singing about her head, as she rode by.

181 ## *Ulysses*

TO the much-tossed Ulysses, never done
    With women whether gowned as wife or whore,
Penelope and Circe seemed as one:
She like a whore made his lewd fancies run,
    And wifely she a hero to him bore.

The counter-changings terrified his way:
    They were the clashing rocks, Symplegades,
Scylla and Charybdis too were they;
Now they were storms frosting the sea with spray
    And now the lotus island's drunken ease.

They multiplied into the Sirens' throng,
    Forewarned by fear of whom he stood bound fast
    Hand and foot helpless to the vessel's mast,
Yet would not stop his ears: daring their song
    He groaned and sweated till that shore was past.

One, two and many: flesh had made him blind,
  Flesh had one pleasure only in the act,
Flesh set one purpose only in the mind—
Triumph of flesh and afterwards to find
  Still those same terrors wherewith flesh was racked.

His wiles were witty and his fame far known,
Every king's daughter sought him for her own,
  Yet he was nothing to be won or lost.
  All lands to him were Ithaca: love-tossed
He loathed the fraud, yet would not bed alone.

182   *The Thieves*

        LOVERS in the act dispense
        With such meum-teum sense
        As might warningly reveal
        What they must not pick or steal,
        And their nostrum is to say:
        'I and you are both away.'

        After, when they disentwine
        You from me and yours from mine,
        Neither can be certain who
        Was that I whose mine was you.
        To the act again they go
        More completely not to know.

        Theft is theft and raid is raid
        Though reciprocally made.
        Lovers, the conclusion is
        Doubled sighs and jealousies
        In a single heart that grieves
        For lost honour among thieves.

AUSTIN CLARKE
1896–

Pilgrimage

(*To my mother*)

WHEN the far south glittered
Behind the grey beaded plains,
And cloudier ships were bitted
Along the pale waves,
The showery breeze—that plies
A mile from Ara—stood
And took our boat on sand:
There by dim wells the women tied
A wish on thorn, while rainfall
Was quiet as the turning of books
In the holy schools at dawn.

Grey holdings of rain
Had grown less with the fields,
As we came to that blessed place
Where hail and honey meet.
O Clonmacnoise was crossed
With light: those cloistered scholars,
Whose knowledge of the gospel
Is cast as metal in pure voices,
Were all rejoicing daily,
And cunning hands with cold and jewels
Brought chalices to flame.

Loud above the grassland,
In Cashel of the towers,
We heard with the yellow candles
The chanting of the hours,
White clergy saying High Mass,
A fasting crowd at prayer,

A choir that sang before them;
And in stained glass the holy day
Was sainted as we passed
Beyond that chancel where the dragons
Are carved upon the arch.

Treasured with chasuble,
Sun-braided, rich-cloak'd wine cup,
We saw, there, iron handbells,
Great annals in the shrine
A high-king bore to battle:
Where, from the branch of Adam,
The noble forms of language—
Brighter than green or blue enamels
Burned in white bronze—embodied
The wings and fiery animals
Which veil the chair of God.

Beyond a rocky townland
And that last tower where ocean
Is dim as haze, a sound
Of wild confession rose:
Black congregations moved
Around the booths of prayer
To hear a saint reprove them;
And from his boat he raised a blessing
To souls that had come down
The holy mountain of the west
Or wailed still in the cloud.

Light in the tide of Shannon
May rise at anchor half
The day and, high in spar-top
Or leather sails of their craft,
Wine merchants will have sleep;

But on a barren isle,
Where Paradise is praised
At daycome, smaller than the seagulls,
We hear white Culdees pray
Until our hollow ship was kneeling
Over the longer waves.

184   *The Planter's Daughter*

WHEN night stirred at sea
And the fire brought a crowd in,
They say that her beauty
Was music in mouth
And few in the candlelight
Thought her too proud,
For the house of the planter
Is known by the trees.

Men that had seen her
Drank deep and were silent,
The women were speaking
Wherever she went—
As a bell that is rung
Or a wonder told shyly,
And O she was the Sunday
In every week.

185   *The Lost Heifer*

WHEN the black herds of the rain were grazing
In the gap of the pure cold wind
And the watery hazes of the hazel
Brought her into my mind,
I thought of the last honey by the water
That no hive can find.

Brightness was drenching through the branches
When she wandered again,
Turning the silver out of dark grasses
Where the skylark had lain,
And her voice coming softly over the meadow
Was the mist becoming rain.

186   *The Straying Student*

On a holy day when sails were blowing southward,
A bishop sang the Mass at Inishmore,
Men took one side, their wives were on the other
But I heard the woman coming from the shore:
And wild in despair my parents cried aloud
For they saw the vision draw me to the doorway.

Long had she lived in Rome when Popes were bad,
The wealth of every age she makes her own,
Yet smiled on me in eager admiration,
And for a summer taught me all I know,
Banishing shame with her great laugh that rang
As if a pillar caught it back alone.

I learned the prouder counsel of her throat,
My mind was growing bold as light in Greece;
And when in sleep her stirring limbs were shown,
I blessed the noonday rock that knew no tree:
And for an hour the mountain was her throne,
Although her eyes were bright with mockery.

228

They say I was sent back from Salamanca
And failed in logic, but I wrote her praise
Nine times upon a college wall in France.
She laid her hand at darkfall on my page
That I might read the heavens in a glance
And I knew every star the Moors had named.

Awake or in my sleep, I have no peace now,
Before the ball is struck, my breath has gone,
And yet I tremble lest she may deceive me
And leave me in this land, where every woman's son
Must carry his own coffin and believe,
In dread, all that the clergy teach the young.

187   *Celebrations*

WHO dare complain or be ashamed
Of liberties our arms have taken?
For every spike upon that gateway,
We have uncrowned the past:
And open hearts are celebrating
Prosperity of church and state
In the shade of Dublin Castle.

So many flagpoles can be seen now
Freeing the crowd, while crisscross keys,
On yellow-and-white above the green,
Treble the wards of nation,
God only knows what treasury
Uncrams to keep each city borough
And thoroughfare in grace.

Let ageing politicians pray
Again, hoardings recount our faith,
The blindfold woman in a rage
Condemn her own for treason:
No steeple topped the scale that Monday,
Rebel souls had lost their savings
And looters braved the street.

188   *Ancient Lights*

WHEN all of us wore smaller shoes
And knew the next world better than
The knots we broke, I used to hurry
On missions of my own by Capel
Street, Bolton Street and Granby Row
To see what man has made. But darkness
Was roomed with fears. Sleep, stripped by woes
I had been taught, beat door, leaped landing,
Lied down the bannister of naught.

Being sent to penance, come Saturday,
I shuffled slower than my sins should.
My fears were candle-spiked at side-shrines,
Rays lengthened them in stained-glass. Confided
To night again, my grief bowed down,
Heard hand on shutter-knob. Did I
Take pleasure, when alone—how much—
In a bad thought, immodest look
Or worse, unnecessary touch?

Closeted in the confessional,
I put on flesh, so many years

Were added to my own, attempted
In vain to keep Dominican
As much i' the dark as I was mixing
Whispered replies with his low words;
Then shuddered past the crucifix,
The feet so hammered, daubed-on blood-drip,
Black with lip-scrimmage of the damned.

Once as I crept from the church-steps,
Beside myself, the air opened
On purpose. Nature read in a flutter
An evening lesson above my head.
Atwirl beyond the leadings, corbels,
A cage-bird came among the sparrows
(The moral inescapable)
Plucked, roof-mired, all in mad bits. O
The pizzicato of its wires!

Goodness of air can be proverbial:
That day, by the kerb at Rutland Square,
A bronze bird fabled out of trees,
Mailing the spearheads of the railings,
Sparrow at nails. I hailed the skies
To save the tiny dropper, found
Appetite gone. A child of clay
Had blustered it away. Pity
Could raise some littleness from dust.

What Sunday clothes can change us now
Or humble orders in black and white?
Stinking with centuries the act
Of thought. So think, man, as that saint
Did, dread the ink-bespattered ex-monk,

And keep your name. No, let me abandon
Night's jakes. Self-persecuted of late
Among the hatreds of rent Europe,
Poetry burns at a different stake.

Still, still I remember awful downpour
Cabbing Mountjoy Street, spun loneliness
Veiling almost the Protestant church,
Two backyards from my very home.
I dared to shelter at locked door.
There, walled by heresy, my fears
Were solved. I had absolved myself:
Feast-day effulgence, as though I gained
For life a plenary indulgence.

The sun came out, new smoke flew up,
The gutters of the Black Church rang
With services. Waste water mocked
The ballcocks: down-pipes sparrowing,
And all around the spires of Dublin
Such swallowing in the air, such cowling
To keep high offices pure: I heard
From shore to shore, the iron gratings
Take half our heavens with a roar.

189   *Marriage*

PARENTS are sinful now, for they must whisper
Too much in the dark. Aye, there's the rub! What grace
Can snatch the small hours from that costly kiss?
Those who slip off the ring, try to be chaste
And when they cannot help it, steal the crumbs
From their own wedding breakfast, spare expense

And keep in warmth the children they have nourished.
But shall the sweet promise of the sacrament
Gladden the heart, if mortals calculate
Their pleasures by the calendar? Night-school
Of love where all, who learn to cheat, grow pale
With guilty hope at every change of moon!

F. R. HIGGINS

1896–1941

190　　　*Padraic O'Conaire,*
　　　　　Gaelic Storyteller

THEY'VE paid the last respects in sad tobacco
And silent is this wakehouse in its haze;
They've paid the last respects; and now their whiskey
Flings laughing words on mouths of prayer and praise;
And so young couples huddle by the gables,
O let them grope home through the hedgy night—
Alone I'll mourn my old friend, while the cold dawn
Thins out the holy candlelight.

Respects are paid to one loved by the people;
Ah, was he not—among our mighty poor—
The sudden wealth cast on those pools of darkness,
Those bearing, just, a star's faint signature;
And so he was to me, close friend, near brother,
Dear Padraic of the wide and sea-cold eyes—
So lovable, so courteous and noble,
The very West was in his soft replies.

They'll miss his heavy stick and stride in Wicklow—
His story-talking down Winetavern Street,
Where old men sitting in the wizen daylight
Have kept an edge upon his gentle wit;
While women on the grassy streets of Galway,
Who hearken for his passing—but in vain,
Shall hardly tell his step as shadows vanish
Through archways of forgotten Spain.

Ah, they'll say: Padraic's gone again exploring;
But now down glens of brightness, O he'll find
An alehouse overflowing with wise Gaelic
That's braced in vigour by the bardic mind,
And there his thoughts shall find their own forefathers—
In minds to whom our heights of race belong,
In crafty men, who ribbed a ship or turned
The secret joinery of song.

Alas, death mars the parchment of his forehead;
And yet for him, I know, the earth is mild—
The windy fidgets of September grasses
Can never tease a mind that loved the wild;
So drink his peace—this grey juice of the barley
Runs with a light that ever pleased his eye—
While old flames nod and gossip on the hearthstone
And only the young winds cry.

191   *Song for the Clatter-bones*

GOD rest that Jewy woman,
Queen Jezebel, the bitch
Who peeled the clothes from her shoulder-bones
Down to her spent teats

234

As she stretched out of the window
Among the geraniums, where
She chaffed and laughed like one half daft
Titivating her painted hair—

King Jehu he drove to her,
She tipped him a fancy beck;
But he from his knacky side-car spoke,
'Who'll break that dewlapped neck?'
And so she was thrown from the window;
Like Lucifer she fell
Beneath the feet of the horses and they beat
The light out of Jezebel.

That corpse wasn't planted in clover;
Ah, nothing of her was found
Save those grey bones that Hare-foot Mike
Gave me for their lovely sound;
And as once her dancing body
Made star-lit princes sweat,
So I'll just clack: though her ghost lacks a back
There's music in the old bones yet.

192   *The Old Jockey*

His last days linger in that low attic
That barely lets out the night,
With its gabled window on Knackers' Alley,
Just hoodwinking the light.

He comes and goes by that gabled window
And then on the window-pane
He leans, as thin as a bottled shadow—
A look, and he's gone again:

235

Eyeing, maybe, some fine fish-women
In the best shawls of the Coombe
Or, maybe, the knife-grinder plying his treadle,
A run of sparks from his thumb!

But, O you should see him gazing, gazing,
When solemnly out on the road
The horse-drays pass overladen with grasses
Each driver lost in his load;

Gazing until they return; and suddenly,
As galloping by they race,
From his pale eyes, like glass breaking,
Light leaps on his face.

193   *The Boyne Walk*

(*To R. M. Smyllie*)

'WHAT's all this rich land,' said I to the Meath man,
'Just mirrors bedazzled with blazing air!'
And like flies on mirrors my parched thoughts ran
As we walked, half-hidden, through where the reeds stand
Between the Boyne and its green canal;
And sweltering I kept to the pace he planned,
Yet he wouldn't even wait in the reeds
To watch a red perch, like a Japanese hand,
Grope in the sun-hot water and weeds—
He merely called back: 'O, go be damned!'

With break-neck looks at the withered end
Of a stupefied town, I paced his heel
By moat, dead wall and under an arch
That was all of a crouch with the weight of the years;

But where the road led I'd have seen—were I wise—
From one running look in the dark of his eyes:
For each seemed the bright astrological plan
Of a new Don Quixote and his man
Again on campaign; but lacking their steeds,
I'd sooner have seen a flick of grey ears
Or a blue lackadaisical eye in the reeds
To lead to a smoky bare back; then cheers!
We'd have ridden our road as the Kings of Meath.

We walked, as became two kings outcast
From plains walled in by a grass-raising lord,
Whose saint is the Joker, whose hope is the Past—
What victuals for bards could that lad afford?
O, none! So off went his dust from our boots,
But his dust that day was of buttercup gold
From a slope, with a sight that was, man alive, grand:
Just two servant girls spreading blue clothes
On grass too deep for a crow to land;
And though they waved to us we kept on our track,
And though to the bank their own clothes soon toppled
We sweltered along—while my thoughts floated back
Through shy beauty's bathing-pool, like an old bottle!

Heat trembled in haloes on grass and on cattle
And each rock blazed like a drunken face;
So I cried to the man of the speedy wattle
'In the name of Lot's wife will you wait a space?
For Adam's red apple hops dry in my throttle,'
And yet instead of easing the pace,
I saw on the broad blackboard of his back
His muscles made signs of a far greater chase,

Until as I tried to keep up on his track
Each pore of my skin became a hot spring
And every bone swam in a blister of pains
While all my bent body seemed as an old crane's
Lost in a great overcoat of wings.

Soon out from my sight off went the big Meath man
Dodging the reeds of his nine-mile road.
So I lolled, as a bard bereft of his dæmon
Or a Moses awaiting a light-burdened cloud;
But heaven lay low all naked and brazen
Within the mad calm on that desert of green,
Where nothing, not even the water, is lean,
Where the orderly touches of Thought aren't seen—
And yet not a wild thought sang in my noddle;
Ah, how could it sing, while speed bit each heel,
While heat tugged a tight noose into my throttle
And while, on my spine, the hung head went nodding
As on it fierce light picked with a black bill.

Then where in soft Meath can one find ease?
When the sun, like a scarecrow, stands in those meadows
Guarding their glory, not even the breeze,
That ghostly rogue, can crop a shadow;
When even I asked for 'A drink, if you please,'
A woman, as proud as a motherly sow,
Hoked out of my way and hid where a larch
Leant like a derrick across an old barge
Stocked in the reeds; and so I went parched!
Ah, but soon down the Boyne, there, O the surprise
From a leaping fish—that silver flicker—
Was nothing compared to what hit my eyes:
An innocent house, marked: 'Licensed for Liquor!'

Could anyone treat me to brighter green meadows
Than the Meath man who finished his thirsty plan when
Between every swig he mooned through those windows?
And yet, on my oath, it was easier then
To coop a mountainy cloud in a henhouse
Than to group the Meath light into lines for my pen;
And still I must bless him since beauty was caught
In ears that were drumming, in eyes all sweat,
In nostrils slimmed by indrawn breath;
For I made, as we lay in the grass by that road
This poem—a gem from the head of a toad;
So here, will you take it—hall-marked by a day
Over the hills and far away?

194 *Father and Son*

ONLY last week, walking the hushed fields
Of our most lovely Meath, now thinned by November,
I came to where the road from Laracor leads
To the Boyne river—that seemed more lake than river,
Stretched in uneasy light and stript of reeds.

And walking longside an old weir
Of my people's, where nothing stirs—only the shadowed
Leaden flight of a heron up the lean air—
I went unmanly with grief, knowing how my father,
Happy though captive in years, walked last with me there.

Yes, happy in Meath with me for a day
He walked, taking stock of herds hid in their own breath-
      ing;
And naming colts, gusty as wind, once steered by his hand,
Lightnings winked in the eyes that were half shy in greeting
Old friends—the wild blades, when he gallivanted the land.

For that proud, wayward man now my heart breaks—
Breaks for that man whose mind was a secret eyrie,
Whose kind hand was sole signet of his race,
Who curbed me, scorned my green ways, yet increasingly
    loved me
Till Death drew its grey blind down his face.

And yet I am pleased that even my reckless ways
Are living shades of his rich calms and passions—
Witnesses for him and for those faint namesakes
With whom now he is one, under yew branches,
Yes, one in a graven silence no bird breaks.

MONK GIBBON

1896–

195 *The Babe*

ONCE my feet trod Nineveh,
Once my eyes saw Troy town burn;
Now, if Plato tells the truth,
Dipped in Lethe I return.

What was old is offered new?
What is new was old before?
That which tired mind evolved
Minds untired may ignore.

Certain now the fields to me
Novel are and unforeseen,
Certain too the neighbouring hedge
A misty miracle of green.

A horse is new, a sheep, a flower,
Bent branch of twig, gnarled trunk of tree,
The lovely and consistent dawn,
The stealthy dusk both new to me.

New from henceforward all that comes,
The prodigal and splendid skies,
A fire's warmth, the first shy glance
Of lover's eyes in lover's eyes.

Every path untrodden yet,
Every sound as yet unheard,
Every thought within the heart
A sleeping thought as yet unstirred.

All to be new—O envious lot!
Most blest of all who nothing knows;
Most rich endowed whose infant mind
Guesses not yet there is the rose.

196 *The Shawls*

THEY'LL walk no longer to Mass on Sunday
In groups or single, sleek-tressed or grey,
The black shawl gathered round head and shoulder,
The shawls are few upon Easter day.

The islands bring them in boat and currach,
Rowing early across the bay,
The bog still clings to its ancient custom,
But the shawls are fewer each Easter day.

Lovely the face that hid its secret,
Lifted in laughter or stooped to pray,
The brow laid bare and the cheek half-curtained,
Till shawls were banished on Easter day.

Had a young girl grace, had she pride of carriage,
Had her glance a meaning, grave or gay,
The shawl revealed it, since naught could hide it,
When they queened it simply some April day.

I met a woman of sixty summers,
Her road before her, a lengthy way,
I turned to stare like a young man dumbstruck—
For the shawl grows rarer from day to day.

That snow-white hair which the brown shawl slipped from,
Those eyes still clear as a sky in May,
That noble forehead, were cause to sorrow
That shawls should vanish this Holy Day.

Is beauty lost, that they hope to purchase
Its shreds and semblance? There were times I'll say
When they stepped it lightly with eyes more flashing,
And hearts more carefree, where joy held sway.

The boats are launching. The Mass is over.
The road is crowded. The sky is grey.
I lingered thinking of heads held higher
When shawls were many—on Easter day.

French Peasants

THESE going home at dusk
Along the lane,
After the day's warm work,
Do not complain.

Were you to say to them,
'What does it mean?
What is it all about,
This troubled dream?'

They would not understand,
They'd go their way
Or, if they spoke at all,
They'd surely say,

'Dawn is the time to rise,
Days are to earn,
Bread and the mid-day rest,
Dusk to return;

'To be content, to pray,
To hear songs sung,
Or to make wayside love,
If one is young.

'All from the good God comes,
All then is good;
Sorrow is known to Him,
And understood.'

One who had questioned all,
And was not wise,
Might be ashamed to meet
Their quiet eyes.

All is so clear to them,
All is so plain,
These who go home at dusk,
Along the lane.

198   *Salt*

OFTEN,
Stepping so delicately through the shrubbery of learning,
The spring mist lighter than a wisp of cloud,
Pearling the leaves and spider-webs with jewels,
Tiptoe, excited, full of hope,
The greedy thumb and index tightly pressed,
But ready in an instant to release
Some grains of less-than-Attic apprehension,
I thought, 'With but a little further zeal she's mine!'
The tracery of her three-toed imprint patterned
Even the mud with tiny hieroglyphics;
And Plato's diligence had brandished once
Handfuls of gem-bright feathers. All was well.
It was delight merely to sniff the morning
And know the wood was haunted by her. Others had said
She hung, in safety caged, above a hundred doorways,
Twittering her daily reassurance.
O mystery of existence, shy as air,
Sometimes a thought, a single phrase, a sentence,
Some intimation not in words at all
But in some earth-borne and earth-bitter fragrance
Seemed to presage for me the ecstatic moment
When, lip to finger, poised for the final step,
I'd launch myself, and with wild joy would feel
Under my hand at last her pulsing heart.
Time was when such hopes were. I did not know
Truth tumbles in the vast and limitless heaven,
Hops, out of reach, a yard or so away,
Or perches in the branch her soul has chosen.

R. N. D. WILSON
1899–1953

Woodcut

A HORSEMAN riding
the wide plains of Eltrim
sees three leagues before him
a great demesne-wall
and windows of a house
the woods have laid siege to.

I watch him from a distance
give the head to his hunter
and take at a gallop
a gap in the stonework
till red coat and chestnut
are lost in the coppice.

Three things October
has shown me this evening,
the first shorn ash-tree
the last swallow gone
and a rider and horse
the woods have laid siege to.

EILEEN SHANAHAN
1901–

The Three Children near Clonmel

I MET three children on the road—
The hawthorn trees were wet with rain
The hills had drawn their white blinds down—
Three children on the road from town.

Their wealthy eyes in splendour mocked
Their faded rags and bare wet feet,
The King had sent his daughters out
To play at peasants in the street.

I could not see the palace walls;
The avenues were dumb with mist;
Perhaps a queen would watch and weep
For lips that she had borne and kissed—

And lost about the lonely world,
With treasury of hair and eye
The tigers of the world will spring,
The merchants of the world will buy.

And one will sell her eyes for gold,
And one will barter them for bread,
And one will watch their glory fade
Beside the looking-glass, unwed.

A hundred years will softly pass,
Yet on the Tipperary hills
The shadows of a king and queen
Will darken on the daffodils.

PATRICK MacDONOGH
1902–

201 *Soon with the Lilac Fades Another Spring*

GOD! but this rain-sweet greenness shakes the heart,
  After untimely drought, after love's lenten fast,
Seeing the tender brightness push apart
  Brown walls of winter. Now to my thoughts at last

Love I have long desired, as grass desires the rain,
   Returns, returns, returns; soft as a settling bird
   Turning itself in the nest, softly her name has stirred,
But oh, this new-sprung joy is all shot through with pain.

This is the selfsame wood whose branches wept
   When Deirdre danced to Naisi, these tall trees
Wound aching arms above while Grainne slept,
   And the immortal changeling Héloïse,
Breaking these brilliant pools with naiad feet,
   Ran to her god, suddenly desolate,
   Remembering Paris and the dark house hushed with hate,
Then the long anguish took them, and the Paraclete.

Soon with the lilac fades another spring,
   And one less left to live, and all our springs must die;
In all the world there lives no lasting thing
   No thing in all the world and you and I,
Mere ghostly springs of summers long since dead,
   Turn to our winter with no second spring—
   I have no solace from remembering
How death's cold hands will hold that arrogant head.

The old men's bat-like voices on the walls
   Were hushed when Helen passed; and even yet
Across three thousand years that shadow falls
   Upon the face of love; for men forget
No beauty branded with the mark of Cain;
   While all the thoughtless-happy fade apace,
   Still the pale virgin in the chapel face
Bids the young eyes of spring witness eternal pain.

202 *She Walked Unaware*

O, SHE walked unaware of her own increasing beauty
That was holding men's thoughts from market or plough,
As she passed by, intent on her womanly duties,
And she without leisure to be wayward or proud;
Or if she had pride then it was not in her thinking
But thoughtless in her body like a flower of good breeding.
The first time I saw her spreading coloured linen
Beyond the green willow she gave me gentle greeting
With no more intention than the leaning willow tree.

Though she smiled without intention yet from that day
   forward
Her beauty filled like water the four corners of my being,
And she rested in my heart like the hare in the form
That is shaped to herself. And I that would be singing
Or whistling at all times went silently then;
Till I drew her aside among straight stems of beeches
When the blackbird was sleeping and promised that never
The fields would be ripe but I'd gather all sweetness,
A red moon of August would rise on our wedding.

October is spreading bright flame along stripped willows
Low fires of the dogwood burn down to grey water,—
God pity me now and all desolate sinners
Demented with beauty! I have blackened my thought
In drouths of bad longing, and all brightness goes shrouded
Since he came with his rapture of wild words that mirrored
Her beauty and made her ungentle and proud.
Tonight she will spread her brown hair on his pillow
But I shall be hearing the harsh cries of wild fowl.

203   *Be Still as You are Beautiful*

BE still as you are beautiful,
    Be silent as the rose;
Through miles of starlit countryside
    Unspoken worship flows
To find you in your loveless room
    From lonely men whom daylight gave
The blessing of your passing face
    Impenetrably grave.

A white owl in the lichened wood
    Is circling silently,
More secret and more silent yet
    Must be your love to me.
Thus, while about my dreaming head
    Your soul in ceaseless vigil goes,
Be still as you are beautiful,
    Be silent as the rose.

204   *The Widow of Drynam*

I STAND in my door and look over the low fields of Dry-
    nam.
No man but the one man has known me, no child but the
    one
Grew big at my breast, and what are my sorrows beside
That pride and that glory? I come from devotions on
    Sunday
And leave them to pity or spite; and though I who had
    music have none

249

But crying of seagulls at morning and calling of curlews at
    night,
I wake and remember my beauty and think of my son
Who would stare the loud fools into silence
And rip the dull parish asunder.

Small wonder indeed he was wild with breeding and beauty
And why would my proud lad not straighten his back from
    the plough?
My son was not got and I bound in a cold bed of duty
Nor led to the side of the road by some clay-clabbered lout!
No, but rapt by a passionate poet away from the dancers
To curtains and silver and firelight,—
O wisely and gently he drew down the pale shell of satin
And all the bright evening's adornment and clad me
Again in the garment of glory, the joy of his eyes.

I stand in my door and look over the low fields of Drynam
When skies move westward, the way he will come from the
    war;
Maybe on a morning of March when a thin sun is shining
And starlings have blackened the thorn,
He will come, my bright limb of glory, my mettlesome
    wild one,
With coin in his pocket and tales on the tip of his tongue,
And the proud ones that slight me will bring back for-
    gotten politeness
To see me abroad on the roads with my son,
The two of us laughing together or stepping in silence.

EARL OF LONGFORD
1902–

(Translations from the Irish)

The Kiss

O H, keep your kisses, young provoking girl!
  I find no taste in any maiden's kiss.
Altho' your teeth be whiter than the pearl,
  I will not drink at fountains such as this.

I know a man whose wife did kiss my mouth
  With kiss more honeyed than the honeycomb.
And never another's kiss can slake my drought
  After that kiss, till judgment hour shall come.

Till I do gaze on her for whom I long,
  If ever God afford such grace to men,
I would not love a woman old or young,
  Till she do kiss me as she kissed me then.

The Careful Husband

I A M told, sir, you're keeping an eye on your wife,
But I can't see the reason for that, on my life.
For if you go out, O most careful of men,
It is clear that you can't keep an eye on her then.

Even when you're at home and take every care,
It is only a waste of your trouble, I swear.
For if you for one instant away from her look,
She'll be off into some inaccessible nook.

If you sit close beside her and don't let her move,
By the flick of an eyelid she'll signal her love.
If you keep her in front of you under your eye,
She will do what she likes and your caution defy.

When she goes out to Mass, as she'd have you suppose,
You must not stay a minute, but go where she goes.
You must not walk in front nor yet too far behind her.
But she's got such a start that I doubt if you'll find her.

JOHN LYLE DONAGHY

1902–47

207   *Voyage*

THIS last October working to a day of sun,
the little spiders that the limp
                      charnel white cocoons
had scattered out of doors, launched all
                on gossamer,
began unpublished daring voyages, taking the quiet
                   road to Samarkand.

Such millions that the silk-covered country
seemed laid with numberless narrow tracks for
                runners.

Next day mid-Autumn wind struck beech and ash.

—O, perishable spinners that have exaggerated
      frailty to fight level with the black,
what hint in nature sent you forth upon the eve
               of storm?

Were your hearts mercury and indexed coming
                  tempest
that you took the last fine evening of the year
to seek your fortune at a gossamer's end?

JOHN LYLE DONAGHY

The sun that flattered the migrating swarm set,
                leaving them in Samarkand,
all but a few, mated, that lowered among the grasses
                whom the gale, next morning, tried.

208   *Duck*

Two wild duck of the upland spaces:
This morning, when the mists had lifted
Half above the bell-noised stream,
They rose in laboured circles, climbing
High into the light, wings plying
Stiffly through the vaporous air;
Till when the victor sun had mounted,
They dropped back into rushy cover.

Noon again, they flew, loud-winged,
This time along a heather byway,
That cuts up to the shallow reaches,
Where they met the secret harm,
Whirled suddenly and fell together,
Fell both beside one clump of rushes,
Dying at the mossy root,
Before the nosing dog had found them.

. . . . . .

A brace of wild duck deftly fettered
The hot hail has done its worst
With sinewy neck, and glossy feathers:
One lies with neck outstretched, eyes staring,
One with head laid under breast,
Both quiet on the old brown dresser.

253

A Leitrim Woman

PEOPLE of Ireland—I am an old woman; I am near my end;
I have lived, now, for seventy-five years in your midst;
I have grown up among you, toiled among you, suffered
    with you and enjoyed with you;
I have given and received in faith and honour;
what was to be endured I have endured, what was to be
    fought against I have fought against, what was to be
    done I have done;
I have married in my country; I have borne two men-
    children and three women-children,
    two sons and three daughters of a Fenian father;
I have brought them up to love and serve Ireland,
    to fight for her to death,
    to work for her at home and abroad,
    to cherish the old glory of Ireland and to strive manfully
    to bring in new light—
    to go forward;
I have brought them up in faith, to know freedom, and love
    justice,
    to take sides with the poor against their spoilers, against
    the leaders who say to a strong class 'Hold all thou
    hast, take all thou canst',
    to unbind heavy burdens and grievous to be borne from
    men's shoulders,
    to render unto the people what is the people's;

I have brought them up to believe in our Lord's prayer,
    to believe in the coming of His Kingdom upon earth and
    to labour that it come indeed;
The strength of my body has gone into the soil of this land,
    and the strength of my children's bodies;

the strength of my soul and the strength of my children's
    soul has been given in the cause of the people of this
    land;
I have suffered, I have endured, when they were in exile
    and in danger of death—
now my husband and one son are dead,
    my last son deported without trial, uncharged—
the spoilers and their friends
the strong and their helpers
    have taken him from me;

I am old, now, and near to death;
those who would have supported me and eased my going
    have been taken from me—
I looked for a little peace before the hour of my departure,
    my last son in the house with me, to see me into the
    grave—
they have driven him forth—
may the curse of heaven, if there be a heaven, light on them;
    the curse of the widow and childless light on them;
    the curse of the poor without advocates,
    the curse of the old without protection,
    the curse of a mother light on them.

RHODA COGHILL

1903–

210   *Runaway*

SOMEBODY must tell me something real
and that very quickly.
Someone must show me a thing
that will not disappear when I touch it,
or fade into a cloud to walk through

when I have looked at it and
thought about it long enough.

You are not final:
you will be bones.
The feet I see marking the pavements
will walk too long
and not long enough,
and I will see the streets
clean in the morning (tomorrow morning) after rain;
but the feet that marked the footpaths
will have stepped into the grave,
stepped into the grave,
before I have done with them.

Who is going to tell me where the dark horses of the spirit go?
Have I come into this room now?
Or was I always in this place?
And could you in your speech
have an inference different from mine?
Do you signify, proud other people,
what you appear to be,
or imply quite another meaning in your existence?

Place me on the edge of a cliff
and tell me now where to leap,
for the horses are pulling on the reins—
I have no wish to hold them.

211   *The Young Bride's Dream*

I WONDER will he still be gentle
When I am fastened safe to his side?
Will he buy grandeur to cover my beauty,
And shelter me like a bird that he'd hide

In a quiet nest, and show me great courtesies,
And make me queen of his body and all that he is?

Or curse me, use me like a chance woman,
A girl that he'd hire at a fair?
Bid me rip my fine gown to a hundred pieces,
Make rags of it then, for the floors and the stair?
I had warning, last night, in a dream without reason or
    rhyme;
But the words may be true ones: '*Obedience is ice to the wine.*'

212   *The Bright Hillside*

WITH a gull's beak I cry
   And mount through strong resistance.
My wingspan beats the sky
   Across the high distance,

Circling about your place,
   Wheeling to cover your bed
With the curve of space
   And the airs overhead;

To keep you, to delay
   Spirit in one dear shape;
But spirit will not stay
   When it has planned escape,

And life at last will leave
   This, and all bodies dead—
Those who remain to grieve:
   The world they habited;

The bushes bared of green,
   The lake waters unfinned,
And the bright hillside clean
   Of any wind.

FRANK O'CONNOR

1903–

(*Translations from the Irish*)

213   *A Grey Eye Weeping*

THAT my old bitter heart was pierced in this black doom,
That foreign devils have made our land a tomb,
That the sun that was Munster's glory has gone down
Has made me a beggar before you, Valentine Brown.

That royal Cashel is bare of house and guest,
That Brian's turreted home is the otter's nest,
That the kings of the land have neither land nor crown
Has made me a beggar before you, Valentine Brown.

Garnish away in the west and her master banned,
Hamburg the refuge of him that has lost his land,
An old grey eye, weeping for lost renown,
Has made me a beggar before you, Valentine Brown.

214   *Kilcash*

WHAT shall we do for timber? The last of the woods is
     down,
Kilcash and the house of its glory and the bell of the house
     are gone,
The spot where that lady waited that shamed all women for
     grace,
When earls came sailing to meet her and Mass was said in
     that place.

My grief and my affliction, your gates are taken away,
Your avenue needs attention, goats in the garden stray,
The courtyard's filled with water, and the great earls
     where are they?
The earls, the lady, the people beaten into the clay.

258

No sound of duck or geese there hawk's cry or eagle's call,
No humming of the bees there that brought honey and
    wax for all,
Nor even the gentle song of the birds there when the sun
    has gone down in the west,
Nor a cuckoo atop of the boughs there, singing the world to
    rest.

There's mist there tumbling from branches unstirred by
    night and by day,
And a darkness falling from heaven, and our fortunes have
    ebbed away;
There's no holly nor hazel nor ash there, the pasture is
    rock and stone,
The crown of the forest is withered and the last of its game
    is gone.

I beseech of Mary and Jesus that the great come home again,
With long dances danced in the garden, fiddle music and
    mirth among men,
That Kilcash, the home of our fathers, be lifted on high again,
And from that to the deluge of waters in bounty and peace
    remain.

EWART MILNE

1903–

215   *Evergreen*

THE signals spelled summer but for me it was spring,
There was talk in the air of how green grew the nation,
And I played with my brothers in a firtree plantation,
The signals spelled summer but for me it was spring.

Cathleen the Countess the country was waking,
Not far were the hills through the eyes of my mother,
The trees in the orchard bore bullets at Easter,
Cathleen the Countess was what they were fruiting.

The signals spelled harvest but for me it was over,
My brothers were scattered and the firtree plantation,
Though the talk still went on of how green grew the
    nation
And the signals spelled harvest, but for me it was over.

In October's reality an image of spring
Restores me and my brothers and the firtree plantation,
Restores Countess and mother and the green of the nation
The October reality, the image of spring.

216   *Could I Believe*

COULD I believe that Death shall die—
As Donne believed—I'd hit the sky!
Could I believe Desire would come
When I desired—I'd speed the sun!
Could I believe the world and love are young
When I feel young—I'd buy a penny whistle and a penny
    drum.

But Death's car roars round corners, roars flat out,
And every night his target for tonight is set;
Then, often dwindles my desire
Unmeshed with any but its own ashy fire;
And when I'd kitten play, or like kid goat bound bold,
A jaundiced world looks on, bald as a vulture, bald and old.

But this I know: that Death shall die
When once I score a hit on him, a real bullseye!
And last night, not in dreams, Desire had come
When I desired—so here's my pipe and drum—
Come dance and sing! Come hither, come hither, come
I'll play for all to whom the world and love are young.

PATRICK KAVANAGH

1905–

217   *Spraying the Potatoes*

THE barrels of blue potato spray
Stood on a headland of July
Beside an orchard wall where roses
Were young girls hanging from the sky.

The flocks of green potato-stalks
Were blossoms spread for sudden flight,
The Kerr's Pinks in a frivelled blue,
The Arran Banners wearing white.

And over that potato field
A lazy veil of woven sun.
Dandelions growing on headlands, showing
Their unloved hearts to everyone.

And I was there with the knapsack sprayer
On the barrel's edge poised. A wasp was floating
Dead on a sunken briar leaf
Over a copper-poisoned ocean.

The axle-roll of a rut-locked cart
Broke the burnt stick of noon in two.
An old man came through a corn-field
Remembering his youth and some Ruth he knew.

He turned my way. 'God further the work.'
He echoed an ancient farming prayer.
I thanked him. He eyed the potatoe drills.
He said: 'You are bound to have good ones there.'

We talked and our talk was a theme of kings
A theme for strings. He hunkered down
In the shade of the orchard wall. O roses
The old man dies in the young girl's frown.

And poet lost to potato-fields,
Remembering the lime and copper smell
Of the spraying barrels he is not lost
Or till blossomed stalks cannot weave a spell.

218   *A Christmas Childhood*

I

ONE side of the potato-pits was white with frost—
How wonderful that was, how wonderful!
And when we put our ears to the paling-post
The music that came out was magical.

The light between the ricks of hay and straw
Was a hole in Heaven's gable. An apple tree
With its December-glinting fruit we saw—
O you, Eve, were the world that tempted me

262

To eat the knowledge that grew in clay
And death the germ within it! Now and then
I can remember something of the gay
Garden that was childhood's. Again

The tracks of cattle to a drinking-place,
A green stone lying sideways in a ditch
Or any common sight the transfigured face
Of a beauty that the world did not touch.

II

My father played the melodeon
Outside at our gate;
There were stars in the morning east
And they danced to his music.

Across the wild bogs his melodeon called
To Lennons and Callans.
As I pulled on my trousers in a hurry
I knew some strange thing had happened.

Outside the cow-house my mother
Made the music of milking;
The light of her stable-lamp was a star
And the frost of Bethlehem made it twinkle.

A water-hen screeched in the bog,
Mass-going feet
Crunched the wafer-ice on the pot-holes,
Somebody wistfully twisted the bellows wheel.

My child poet picked out the letters
On the grey stone,
In silver the wonder of a Christmas townland,
The winking glitter of a frosty dawn.

Cassiopeia was over
Cassidy's hanging hill,
I looked and three whin bushes rode across
The horizon—the Three Wise Kings.

An old man passing said:
'Can't he make it talk'—
The melodeon. I hid in the doorway
And tightened the belt of my box-pleated coat.

I nicked six nicks on the door-post
With my penknife's big blade—
There was a little one for cutting tobacco.
And I was six Christmases of age.

My father played the melodeon,
My mother milked the cows,
And I had a prayer like a white rose pinned
On the Virgin Mary's blouse.

219 *Epic*

I HAVE lived in important places, times
When great events were decided: who owned
That half a rood of rock, a no-man's land
Surrounded by our pitchfork-armed claims.
I heard the Duffys shouting 'Damn your soul'
And old McCabe stripped to the waist, seen
Step the plot defying blue cast-steel—
'Here is the march along these iron stones'
That was the year of the Munich bother. Which
Was most important? I inclined
To lose my faith in Ballyrush and Gortin
Till Homer's ghost came whispering to my mind
He said: I made the Iliad from such
A local row. Gods make their own importance.

Pegasus

My soul was an old horse
Offered for sale in twenty fairs.
I offered him to the Church—the buyers
Were little men who feared his unusual airs.
One said: 'Let him remain unbid
In the wind and rain and hunger
Of sin and we will get him—
With the winkers thrown in—for nothing.'

Then the men of State looked at
What I'd brought for sale.
One minister, wondering if
Another horse-body would fit the tail
That he'd kept for sentiment—
The relic of his own soul—
Said, 'I will graze him in lieu of his labour.'
I lent him for a week or more
And he came back a hurdle of bones,
Starved, overworked, in despair.
I nursed him on the roadside grass
To shape him for another fair.

I lowered my price. I stood him where
The broken-winded, spavined stand
And crooked shopkeepers said that he
Might do a season on the land—
But not for high-paid work in towns.
He'd do a tinker, possibly.
I begged, 'O make some offer now,
A soul is a poor man's tragedy.

He'll draw your dungiest cart,' I said,
'Show you short cuts to Mass,
Teach weather lore, at night collect
Bad debts from poor men's grass.'
  And they would not.

 Where the
Tinkers quarrel I went down
With my horse, my soul.
I cried, 'Who will bid me half a crown?'
From their rowdy bargaining
Not one turned. 'Soul,' I prayed,
'I have hawked you through the world
Of Church and State and meanest trade.
But this evening, halter off,
Never again will it go on.
On the south side of ditches
There is grazing of the sun.
No more haggling with the world. . . .'

As I said these words he grew
Wings upon his back. Now I may ride him
Every land my imagination knew.

221 *Memory of Brother Michael*

I T would never be morning, always evening,
Golden sunset, golden age—
When Shakespeare, Marlowe and Jonson were writing
The future of England page by page
A nettle-wild grave was Ireland's stage.

It would never be spring, always autumn,
After a harvest always lost,
When Drake was winning seas for England
We sailed in puddles of the past
Chasing the ghost of Brendan's mast.

The seeds among the dust were less than dust,
Dust we sought, decay,
The young sprout rising, smothered in it,
Cursed for being in the way—
And the same is true to-day.

Culture is always something that was,
Something pedants can measure,
Skull of bard, thigh of chief,
Depth of dried-up river.
Shall we be thus forever?
Shall we be thus forever?

222   *Shancoduff*

MY black hills have never seen the sun rising
Eternally they look north towards Armagh.
Lot's wife would not be salt if she had been
Incurious as my black hills that are happy
When dawn whitens Glassdrummond chapel.

My hills hoard the bright shillings of March
While the sun searches in every pocket.
They are my Alps and I have climbed the Matterhorn
With a sheaf of hay for three perishing calves
In the field under the Big Forth of Rocksavage.

The sleety winds fondle the rushy beards of Shancoduff
While the cattle-drovers sheltering in the Featherna Bush
Look up and say: 'Who owns them hungry hills
That the water-hen and snipe must have forsaken?
A poet? Then by heavens he must be poor.'
I hear and is my heart not badly shaken?

223   *Auditors in*

I

THE problem that confronts me here
Is to be eloquent yet sincere;
Let myself rip and not go phoney
In an inflated testimony.
Is verse an entertainment only?
Or is it a profound and holy
Faith that cries the inner history
Of the failure of man's mission?
Should it be my job to mention
Precisely how I chanced to fail
Through a cursed ideal.
Write down here: he knew what he wanted—
Evilest knowledge ever haunted
Man when he can picture clear
Just what he is searching for.

A car, a big suburban house,
Half secret that he might not lose
The wild attraction of the poor.
But proud, the fanatic lure
For women of the poet's way
And diabolic underlay;

The gun of pride can bring them down
At twenty paces in the town—
For what? the tragedy is this
Pride's gunman hesitates to kiss:
A romantic Rasputin
Praying at the heart of sin.
He cannot differentiate
Say if he does not want to take
From moral motives or because
Nature has ideal in her laws.
But to get down to the factual—
You are not homosexual.
And yet you live without a wife,
A most disorganised sort of life.
You've not even bred illegitimates
A lonely lecher whom the fates
By a financial trick castrates.
You're capable of an intense
Love that is experience.
Remember how your heart was moved
And youth's eternity was proved
When you saw a young girl going to Mass
On a weekday morning as
You yourself used to go
Down to the Church from Ednamo.
Your imagination still enthuses
Over the dandelions at Willie Hughes'
And these are equally valid
For urban epic, peasant ballad.
Not mere memory but the Real
Poised in the poet's commonweal.
And you must take yourself in hand
And dig and ditch your authentic land.

Wake up, wake up and compromise
On the non-essential sides
Love's round you in a rapturous bevy
But you are bankrupt by the levy
Imposed upon the ideal:
Her Cheshire-cat smile surmounts the wall.
She smiles 'Wolf, wolf, come be my lover'.

II

After the prayer I am ready to enter my heart
Indifferent to the props of a reputation:
Some feeble sallies of a peasant plantation,
The rotten shafts of a remembered cart
Holding up the conscious crust of art.
No quiet corner here for contemplation,
No roots of faith to give my angry passion
Validity. I at the bottom will start
Try to ignore the shame-reflecting eyes
Of worshippers who made their god too tall
To share their food or do the non-stupendous,
They gave him for exploring empty skies
Instead of a little room where he might write for
Men too real to live by vapid legends.

Away, away, away on wings like Joyce's
Mother Earth is putting my brand new clothes in order
Praying, she says, that I no more ignore her
Yellow buttons she found in fields at bargain prices.
Kelly's Big Bush for a button-hole. Surprises
In every pocket—the stream at Connolly's corner
Myself at Annavackey on the Armagh border
Or calm and collected in a calving crisis

Not sad at all as I float away away
With Mother keeping me to the vernacular.
I have a home to return to now. O blessing
For the Return in Departure. Somewhere to stay
Doesn't matter. What is distressing
Is waking eagerly to go nowhere in particular.

From the sour soil of a town where all roots canker
I turn away to where the Self reposes
The placeless Heaven that's under all our noses
Where we're shut off from all the barren anger
No time for self-pitying melodrama
A million Instincts know no other uses
Than all day long to feed and charm the Muses
Till they become pure positive. O hunger
Where all have mouths of desire and none
Is willing to be eaten! I am so glad
To come so accidentally upon
My Self at the end of a tortuous road
And have learned with surprise that God
Unworshipped withers to the Futile One.

C. DAY-LEWIS

1905–

224

The Poet

FOR me there is no dismay
Though ills enough impend.
I have learned to count each day
Minute by breathing minute—
Birds that lightly begin it,
Shadows muting its end—

As lovers count for luck
Their own heart-beats and believe
In the forest of time they pluck
Eternity's single leaf.

Tonight the moon's at the full.
Full moon's the time for murder.
But I look at the clouds that hide her—
The bay below me is dull,
An unreflecting glass—
And chafe for the clouds to pass,
And wish she suddenly might
Blaze down at me so I shiver
Into a twelve-branched river
Of visionary light.

For now imagination,
My royal, impulsive swan,
With raking flight—I can see her—
Comes down as it were upon
A lake in whirled snow-floss
And flurry of spray like a skier
Checking. Again I feel
The wounded waters heal.
Never before did she cross
My heart with such exaltation.

Oh, on this striding edge,
This hare-bell height of calm
Where intuitions swarm
Like nesting gulls and knowledge
Is free as the winds that blow,
A little while sustain me,
Love, till my answer is heard!

Oblivion roars below,
Death's cordon narrows: but vainly,
If I've slipped the carrier word.

Dying, any man may
Feel wisdom harmonious, fateful
At the tip of his dry tongue.
All I have felt or sung
Seems now but the moon's fitful
Sleep on a clouded bay,
Swan's maiden flight, or the climb
To a tremulous, hare-bell crest.
Love, tear the song from my breast!
Short, short is the time.

225   *Jig*

THAT winter love spoke and we raised no objection, at
Easter 'twas daisies all light and affectionate,
June sent us crazy for natural selection—not
Four traction-engines could tear us apart.
Autumn then coloured the map of our land,
Oaks shuddered and apples came ripe to the hand,
In the gap of the hills we played happily, happily,
Even the moon couldn't tell us apart.

Grave winter drew near and said, 'This will not do at all—
If you continue, I fear you will rue it all.'
So at the New Year we vowed to eschew it
Although we both knew it would break our heart.
But spring made hay of our good resolutions—
Lovers, you may be as wise as Confucians,
Yet once love betrays you he plays you and plays you
Like fishes for ever, so take it to heart.

226 *Do not Expect Again a Phoenix Hour*

Do not expect again a phoenix hour,
The triple-towered sky, the dove complaining,
Sudden the rain of gold and heart's first ease
Tranced under trees by the eldritch light of sundown.

By a blazed trail our joy will be returning:
One burning hour throws light a thousand ways,
And hot blood stays into familiar gestures.
The best years wait, the body's plenitude.

Consider then, my lover, this is the end
Of the lark's ascending, the hawk's unearthly hover:
Spring season is over soon and first heatwave;
Grave-browed with cloud ponders the huge horizon.

Draw up the dew. Swell with pacific violence.
Take shape in silence. Grow as the clouds grew.
Beautiful brood the cornlands, and you are heavy;
Leafy the boughs—they also hide big fruit.

227 *The Album*

I SEE you, a child
In a garden sheltered for buds and playtime,
Listening as if beguiled
By a fancy beyond your years and the flowering maytime.
The print is faded: soon there will be
No trace of that pose enthralling,
Nor visible echo of my voice distantly calling
'Wait! Wait for me!'

Then I turn the page
To a girl who stands like a questioning iris
By the waterside, at an age
That asks every mirror to tell what the heart's desire is.
The answer she finds in that oracle stream
Only time could affirm or disprove,
Yet I wish I were there to venture a warning, 'Love
Is not what you dream.'

Next you appear
As if garlands of wild felicity crowned you—
Courted, caressed, you wear
Like immortelles the lovers and friends around you.
'They will not last you, rain or shine,
They are but straws and shadows,'
I cry: 'Give not to those charming desperadoes
What was made to be mine.'

One picture is missing—
The last. It would show me a tree stripped bare
By intemperate gales, her amazing
Noonday of blossom spoilt which promised so fair.
Yet, scanning those scenes at your heyday taken,
I tremble, as one who must view
In the crystal a doom he could never deflect—yes, I too
Am fruitlessly shaken.

I close the book;
But the past slides out of its leaves to haunt me
And it seems, wherever I look,
Phantoms of irreclaimable happiness taunt me.
Then I see her, petalled in new-blown hours,
Beside me—'All you love most there
Has blossomed again,' she murmurs, 'all that you missed there
Has grown to be yours.'

228   *But Two There Are . . .*

BUT two there are, shadow us everywhere
And will not let us be till we are dead,
Hardening the bones, keeping the spirit spare,
Original in water, earth and air,
Our bitter cordial, our daily bread.

Turning over old follies in ante-room:
For first-born waiting or for late reprieve,
Watching the safety-valve, the slackening loom,
Abed, abroad, at every turn and tomb
A shadow starts, a hand is on your sleeve.

O you, my comrade, now or tomorrow flayed
Alive, crazed by the nibbling nerve; my friend
Whom hate has cornered or whom love betrayed,
By hunger sapped, trapped by a stealthy tide,
Brave for so long but whimpering in the end:

Such are the temporal princes, fear and pain,
Whose borders march with the ice-fields of death,
And from that servitude escape there's none
Till in the grave we set up house alone
And buy our liberty with our last breath.

229   *Statuette: Late Minoan*

GIRL of the musing mouth,
The mild archaic air,
For whom do you subtly smile?
Yield to what power or prayer
Breasts vernally bare?

I seem to be peering at you
Through the wrong end of time
That shrinks to a bright, far image—
Great Mother of earth's prime—
A stature sublime.

So many golden ages
Of sunshine steeped your clay,
So dear did the maker cherish
In you life's fostering ray,
That you warm us to-day.

Goddess or girl, you are earth.
The smile, the offered breast—
They were the dream of one
Thirsting as I for rest,
As I, unblest.

BRYAN GUINNESS

1905–

230   *The Summer is Coming*

THE summer is coming
Over the hills;
The milk of the blackthorn
Is bursting and spills;
All day the cuckoo
In County Mayo
Breathes like a flute
As he flits high and low.

Dark is the turf
And grey is the stone,
And sad is the sky
For the wild geese gone;
But the gleaming cloak
Of the grass begins
Under the golden
Brooch of the whins.

The black boats walk
On the silver strand,
Like beetles that go
On the edge of the land;
The black boats tilt
On the western waves;
Black heifers stand over
The old green graves.

Summer is coming
Over the sea
And lights with soft kisses
On you and on me;
All day the cuckoo
In County Mayo
Breathes like a flute
As he flits high and low.

231   *What Are They Thinking . . .*

WHAT are they thinking, the people in churches,
Closing their eyelids and kneeling to pray,
Touching their faces and sniffing their fingers,
Folding their knuckles one over another?
What are they thinking? Do they remember

This is the church: and this is the steeple:
Open the door: and here are the people?
Do they still see the parson climbing upstairs,
Opening the window and saying his prayers?
Do they perceive in the pit of their palms
The way of the walls and the spin of the spire,
The turmoil of tombstones tossed in the grass,
Under the yawning billows of yew?
Can they discover, drooping beyond them,
The chestnuts' fountains of flowers and frills,
And the huge fields folded into the hills?

What are they thinking, the sheep on the hills,
Bobbing and bending to nibble the grass,
Kissing the crisp green coat of the combes?
What are they thinking, lying contented
With vacant regard in long rumination?
Do they consider the sky as a cage,
Their fleeces as fetters, their bones as their bonds?
Or do they rejoice at the thyme on their tongues,
The dome of the sky, the slope of the downs,
The village below, the church, and the steeple,
With shepherd and ploughman and parson and people?

And what is he feeling, the lark as he flies,
Does he consider the span of his days,
Does he dissever himself from his spirit,
His flight from his feathers, his song from his singing?
Is he cast down at the thought of his brevity?
Or does he look forward to fond immortality?
He stitches the sky with the thread of his breath
To all the bright pattern of living beneath,
To ploughman and shepherd and parson and people,
To the sheep on the hills and the church and the steeple.

SHEILA WINGFIELD

1906–

232   *Odysseus Dying*

I THINK Odysseus, as he dies, forgets
Which was Calypso, which Penelope,
Only remembering the wind that sets
Off Mimas, and how endlessly
His eyes were stung with brine;
Argos a puppy, leaping happily;
And his old Father digging round a vine.

PADRAIC FALLON

1906–

233   *The Waistcoat*

O RO, the islandmen
Load herring from the white shoals
Into the barrows of the shawled fishwives
On the grey wall of Galway:
And lightly where sunlight was warehoused by the water
From the tarred hulls they sway
In their blue homespuns and skin shoes
To the hazy wall and away.

O tell me what lazy Peeler
Thumbing his girth will dare them
Now money that ripens like rain on ropes
Runs down their hasty fingers?
And what fat terrified son of the devil
That tends a till won't pull back porter
All night for men whose eyes make knives
Of the lights that worm through his bottled windows?

But quietly at last as a sheep-fair
From the old square the day disperses,
One spark of the sun stands hitched
Like a lonely ram in a corner,
And Padraic the son of Patcheen Rua
Shakes the drink from the wild top of his skull
And stoops from the door in his whispering shoes
To dandle the sky on his shoulder.

O grey city
Of stone and mist and water,
Here's terror, a son of Clan Flaherty
Footloose in your sleepy air.
Have you no shocked sudden memory
Of rape and ringing steeple
As he grows in a lane, towering, till the sea
Seems no more size than a mackerel?

Fly for the bishop, quick.
Call all the lazy constables for, O,
By Padraic Patcheen Rua now
An innocent woman idles.
Bright in the midnight of her shawl
Her face rises, in her own light
Her piled hair slipping from the comb
Could hide a lover out of sight.

O, Padraic Patcheen Rua, such a woman
Never had a match
In any thatched house on the windy island;
And, O, Padraic, did she stretch
On the top of a headland with you of an evening
What riches your great hand would win
Burning on all her slow horizons down
From crown to shin.

Man, dear, do you dawdle
And the world before you?
A ship with two sails
And a gallow's crew,
And the wind right for Connemara
Where you will have your will
And potheen in a jug
By a three-legged stool?

Open your mouth, O dolt.
Strike the great silver string.
Give the gossips a story, we sicken
Of talking of tides and fish.
Lay hands on her, show her the rocks
And rainbows of water we twist
Out of ourselves for the women, bringing
An ocean on the bowsprit.

Are you making a mock of us, Padraic?
Is an islandman backing
Round like a colt if a woman
But finger his elbow?
By God, do you turn and run
And she trying to hold you
So hard that you leave in her two hands
Three parts of your woollen waistcoat?

O, your wife will magnify you
To our wives at the chapel door.
And a hundred and twenty-seven saints whose bones
Are green grass in Killeaney
Will praise you with praises flashing on the eaves
Of heaven like wintry drops of rain.
But what of us, Padraic, what of us,
Men raised to the sea?

What of the men who tie the wind in ropes
And lead the sea horses by little bridles?
What of us who catch fish
In shudders of black starlight?
What will the noisy fishwomen cry from the wall
As we creep out towards the sky?
Ah, Padraic, I who tell the story
Cover my face and sigh.

234   *Mary Hynes*

(*After the Irish of Raftery*)

THAT Sunday, on my oath, the rain was a heavy overcoat
On a poor poet, and when the rain began
In fleeces of water to buckleap like a goat
I was only a walking penance reaching Kiltartan;
And there, so suddenly that my cold spine
Broke out on the arch of my back in a rainbow,
This woman surged out of the day with so much sunlight
I was nailed there like a scarecrow,

But I found my tongue and the breath to balance it
And I said: 'If I bow to you with this hump of rain
I'll fall on my collarbone, but look, I'll chance it,
And after falling, bow again.'
She laughed, ah, she was gracious, and softly she said to me,
'For all your lovely talking I go marketing with an ass,
I'm no hill-queen, alas, or Ireland, that grass widow,
So hurry on, sweet Raftery, or you'll keep me late for
    Mass!'

The parish priest has blamed me for missing second Mass
And the bell talking on the rope of the steeple,
But the tonsure of the poet is the bright crash
Of love that blinds the irons on his belfry,
Were I making an Aisling I'd tell the tale of her hair,
But now I've grown careful of my listeners
So I pass over one long day and the rainy air
Where we sheltered in whispers.

When we left the dark evening at last outside her door,
She lighted a lamp though a gaming company
Could have sighted each trump by the light of her un-
    shawled poll,
And indeed she welcomed me
With a big quart bottle and I mooned there over glasses
Till she took that bird, the phœnix, from the spit;
And 'Raftery,' says she, 'a feast is no bad dowry,
Sit down now and taste it!'

If I praised Ballylea before it was only for the mountains
Where I broke horses and ran wild,
And not for its seven crooked smoky houses
Where seven crones are tied
All day to the listening top of a half door,
And nothing to be heard or seen
But the drowsy dropping of water
And a gander on the green.

But, Boys! I was blind as a kitten till last Sunday.
This town is earth's very navel!
Seven palaces are thatched there of a Monday,
And O the seven queens whose pale

Proud faces with their seven glimmering sisters,
The Pleiads, light the evening where they stroll,
And one can find the well by their wet footprints,
And make one's soul;

For Mary Hynes, rising, gathers up there
Her ripening body from all the love stories;
And, rinsing herself at morning, shakes her hair
And stirs the old gay books in libraries;
And what shall I do with sweet Boccaccio?
And shall I send Ovid back to school again
With a new headline for his copybook,
And a new pain?

Like a nun she will play you a sweet tune on a spinet,
And from such grasshopper music leap
Like Herod's hussy who fancied a saint's head
For grace after meat;
Yet she'll peg out a line of clothes on a windy morning
And by noonday put them ironed in the chest,
And you'll swear by her white fingers she does nothing
But take her fill of rest.

And I'll wager now that my song is ended,
Loughrea, that old dead city where the weavers
Have pined at the mouldering looms since Helen broke the
    thread,
Will be piled again with silver fleeces:
O the new coats and big horses! The raving and the
    ribbons!
And Ballylea in hubbub and uproar!
And may Raftery be dead if he's not there to ruffle it
On his own mare, Shank's mare, that never needs a spur!

But ah, Sweet Light, though your face coins
My heart's very metals, isn't it folly without pardon
For Raftery to sing so that men, east and west, come
Spying on your vegetable garden?
We could be so quiet in your chimney corner—
Yet how could a poet hold you any more than the sun,
Burning in the big bright hazy heart of harvest,
Could be tied in a henrun?

Bless your poet then and let him go!
He'll never stack a haggard with his breath:
His thatch of words will not keep rain or snow
Out of the house, or keep back death.
But Raftery, rising, curses as he sees you
Stir the fire and wash delph,
That he was bred a poet whose selfish trade it is
To keep no beauty to himself.

235 *The River Walk*

DISTURBING it is
To take your stick sedately talking,
Evening in the water and the air;
And discover this: that a woman is a river.
The mythic properties are hard to bear.

Dismaying are
The ways she will intrude—if she intrude
Or merely assume the garments that you give her:
But a water willow stared at for so long
Glows graciously and knows the why you brood.

And such gesticulation—
Are you so young?—before the gentle birch
In its first shimmer: Lover, are you true
To one, or merely finding all you search
Brings the one woman home to you?

But how absurd to see
Her in that stilted bird, the heron in
A silt of river, all her blues pinned up:
In that brocaded goose the swan
For all her myths with Jupiter on top.

Dangerous, dangerous
This mythology. The doctors know it
And reason of it now like any poet.
Lover, go back no farther than your birth:
A woman is a woman, not the earth.

Her human business is
To resolve a man of other women always,
Not be, in a beautiful grotesque, all bodies
So various, a lover—if the girl insist
On love—must be a very pantheist.

236   *Farmer*

LAST winter a Snowman; and after snow an Iceman
Shattering, O cold, his bright blue limbs like glass
With every frozen footstep; in the thaws that followed on,
A doll that almost melted into mud without a face.

What of it. The sun's in his hands now, hands of iron
That run too with the soft spark of clay,
His look is mild and large as the horizon,
He loses himself in the earth like a summer day.

But how he will come to you, woman, gathering up
His body in a thunder off the grass
In a four-legged gust, he's away and over the fields a pace—
Tallyho, tallyho—with the whole wild earth at a gallop:
Just beckon, he'll roar up like weather, only to sway
So softly down you'll think him the month of May.

LOUIS MacNEICE

1907–

237   *The Sunlight on the Garden*

THE sunlight on the garden
Hardens and grows cold,
We cannot cage the minute
Within its nets of gold,
When all is told
We cannot beg for pardon.

Our freedom as free lances
Advances towards its end;
The earth compels, upon it
Sonnets and birds descend;
And soon, my friend,
We shall have no time for dances.

The sky was good for flying
Defying the church bells
And every evil iron
Siren and what it tells:
The earth compels,
We are dying, Egypt, dying

And not expecting pardon,
Hardened in heart anew,
But glad to have sat under
Thunder and rain with you,
And grateful too
For sunlight on the garden.

238   *Dublin*

GREY brick upon brick,
Declamatory bronze
On sombre pedestals—
O'Connell, Grattan, Moore—
And the brewery tugs and the swans
On the balustraded stream
And the bare bones of a fanlight
Over a hungry door
And the air soft on the cheek
And porter running from the taps
With a head of yellow cream
And Nelson on his pillar
Watching his world collapse.

This was never my town,
I was not born nor bred
Nor schooled here and she will not
Have me alive or dead
But yet she holds my mind
With her seedy elegance,
With her gentle veils of rain
And all her ghosts that walk
And all that hide behind
Her Georgian façades—

The catcalls and the pain,
The glamour of her squalor,
The bravado of her talk.

The lights jig in the river
With a concertina movement
And the sun comes up in the morning
Like barley-sugar on the water
And the mist on the Wicklow hills
Is close, as close
As the peasantry were to the landlord,
As the Irish to the Anglo-Irish,
As the killer is close one moment
To the man he kills,
Or as the moment itself
Is close to the next moment.

She is not an Irish town
And she is not English,
Historic with guns and vermin
And the cold renown
Of a fragment of Church latin,
Of an oratorical phrase.
But O the days are soft,
Soft enough to forget
The lesson better learnt,
The bullet on the wet
Streets, the crooked deal,
The steel behind the laugh,
The Four Courts burnt.

Fort of the Dane,
Garrison of the Saxon,
Augustan capital
Of a Gaelic nation,

Appropriating all
The alien brought,
You give me time for thought
And by a juggler's trick
You poise the toppling hour—
O greyness run to flower,
Grey stone, grey water
And brick upon grey brick.

239   *Galway*

O the crossbones of Galway,
The hollow grey houses,
The rubbish and sewage,
The grass-grown pier,
And the dredger grumbling
All night in the harbour:
The war came down on us here.

Salmon in the Corrib
Gently swaying
And the water combed out
Over the weir
And a hundred swans
Dreaming on the harbour:
The war came down on us here.

The night was gay
With the moon's music
But Mars was angry
On the hills of Clare
And September dawned
Upon willows and ruins:
The war came down on us here.

Prognosis

GOODBYE, Winter,
The days are getting longer,
The tea-leaf in the teacup
Is herald of a stranger.

Will he bring me business
Or will he bring me gladness
Or will he come for cure
Of his own sickness?

With a pedlar's burden
Walking up the garden
Will he come to beg
Or will he come to bargain?

Will he come to pester,
To cringe or to bluster,
A promise in his palm
Or a gun in his holster?

Will his name be John
Or will his name be Jonah
Crying to repent
On the Island of Iona?

Will his name be Jason
Looking for a seaman
Or a mad crusader
Without rhyme or reason?

What will be his message—
War or work or marriage?
News as new as dawn
Or an old adage?

Will he give a champion
Answer to my question
Or will his words be dark
And his ways evasion?

Will his name be Love,
And all his talk be crazy?
Or will his name be Death
And his message easy?

241 *Christina*

IT all began so easy
With bricks upon the floor
Building motley houses
And knocking down your houses
And always building more.

The doll was called Christina,
Her underwear was lace,
She smiled while you dressed her
And when you then undressed her
She kept a smiling face.

Until the day she tumbled
And broke herself in two
And her legs and arms were hollow
Behind her eyes of blue.

. . . . .

He went to bed with a lady
Somewhere seen before,
He heard the name Christina
And suddenly saw Christina
Dead on the nursery floor.

Cradle Song

SLEEP, my darling, sleep;
   The pity of it all
Is all we compass if
   We watch disaster fall.
Put off your twenty-odd
   Encumbered years and creep
Into the only heaven,
   The robbers' cave of sleep.

The wild grass will whisper,
   Lights of passing cars
Will streak across your dreams
   And fumble at the stars;
Life will tap the window
   Only too soon again,
Life will have her answer—
   Do not ask her when.

When the winsome bubble
   Shivers, when the bough
Breaks, will be the moment
   But not here or now.
Sleep and, asleep, forget
   The watchers on the wall
Awake all night who know
   The pity of it all.

DENIS DEVLIN

1908–

243 ## *The Tomb of Michael Collins*

(*To Ignazio Silone*)

I

MUCH I remember of the death of men,
But his I most remember, most of all,
More than the familiar and forgetful
Ghosts who leave our memory too soon—
Oh, what voracious fathers bore him down!

It was all sky and heather, wet and rock,
No one was there but larks and stiff-legged hares
And flowers bloodstained. Then, Oh, our shame so massive
Only a God embraced it and the angel
Whose hurt and misty rifle shot him down.

One by one the enemy dies off;
As the sun grows old, the dead increase,
We love the more the further from we're born!
The bullet found him where the bullet ceased,
And Gael and Gall went inconspicuous down.

II

There are the Four Green Fields we loved in boyhood,
There are some reasons it's no loss to die for:
Even it's no loss to die for having lived;
It is inside our life the angel happens
Life, the gift that God accepts or not,

Which Michael took with hand, with harsh, grey eyes,
He was loved by women and by men,
He fought a week of Sundays and by night
He asked what happened and he knew what was—
O Lord! how right that them you love die young!

He's what I was when by the chiming river
Two loyal children long ago embraced—
But what I was is one thing, what remember
Another thing, how memory becomes knowledge—
Most I remember him, how man is courage.

And sad, Oh sad, that glen with one thin stream
He met his death in; and a farmer told me
There was but one small bird to shoot: it sang
'Better Beast and know your end, and die
Than Man with murderous angels in his head.'

III

I tell these tales—I was twelve-year-old that time.
Those of the past were heroes in my mind:
Edward the Bruce whose brother Robert made him
Of Ireland, King; Wolfe Tone and Silken Thomas
And Prince Red Hugh O'Donnell most of all.

The newsboys knew and the apple and orange women
Where was his shifty lodging Tuesday night;
No one betrayed him to the foreigner,
No Protestant or Catholic broke and ran
But murmured in their heart: here was a man!

Then came that mortal day he lost and laughed at,
He knew it as he left the armoured car;
The sky held in its rain and kept its breath;
Over the Liffey and the Lee, the gulls,
They told his fortune which he knew, his death.

Walking to Vespers in my Jesuit school,
The sky was come and gone; 'O Captain, my Captain!'
Walt Whitman was the lesson that afternoon—
How sometimes death magnifies him who dies,
And some, though mortal, have achieved their race.

The Colours of Love

I

WOMEN that are loved are more than lovable,
  Their beauty absolute blows:
But wastes away the urgent, carnal soul
  More than its leaves so mortal in the rose.

O rose! O more than red mortality!
  What can my love have said
That made her image more than be?
  Her mind more than mind, blood more than red?

II

Those beautiful women shone against the dark
With flowers upon the breast, and birds
Disturbed by foreknowledge, sang some notes.
There were unshed tears, reproach and fret;
I wondered if their women's time was yet.

And the flowers like milk in a dark pantry at night
Offered themselves to the groping hand;
The cliffs fell faster than tears
Reaching that pain where feeling does not matter;
Nor through the house the ghosts' averse patter,

Repeating their old theme of the unknown
Birds or women never did translate:
It was as if eternity were breathing
Through the small breathing of the flowers
Shining upon its breast with speechless light.

III

It cannot well be said of love and death
That love is better and that death is worse,
Unless we buy death off with loving breath
So he may rent his beauty with our purse.

But is that beauty, is that beauty death?
No, it's the mask by which we're drawn to him,
It is with our consent death finds his breath;
Love is death's beauty and annexes him.

IV

At the *Bar du Départ* drink farewell
And say no word you'll be remembered by;
Nor Prince nor President can ever tell
Where love ends or when it does or why.

Down the boulevard the lights come forth
Like my rainflowers trembling all through Spring,
Blue and yellow in the Celtic North . . .
The stone's ripple weakens, ring by ring.

Better no love than love, which, through loving
Leads to no love. The ripples come to rest . . .
Ah me! how all that young year I was moving
To take her dissolution to my breast!

FRANCIS MacMANUS
1909–

245 *Pattern of Saint Brendan*

THIS is an evening for a hallowed landfall.
The land breeze slithers down Brandon
Mountain, where stone on stone the monkhives
topple and no prayers drone since twelve evangels
voyaged to find the summer islands.
The light withdraws over the maudlin village
and upended currachs humped like black cattle,
to follow the copper Atlantic shimmer.
O now could twelve exiles
return from voyaging, staring at wonders and charting
infinity, and raise dripping oars to glide
rejoicing, chanting *laudate* with salty lips cracking,
back from the peril of where the sun founders,
to search for lost Ireland round their cold mountain.

This is the evening. The bleat of melodeons
buckleaps fandangos and whips
up the hobnails to belt at the floorboards.
Thirst gravels the gullet; lads with puffed faces
muster a yowl for slopped foamy porter
and grope for the pence in first-hoarded purses.
Fug blears the wicks; the sergeant is strutting,
tunic neck-open, bellyband bursting;
Annastatia and Nellie slip off to go pairing
at a tip and a wink to the back of the graveyard.
Goat-music, fumes, the stamp of wild heel-bones,
dust whirling high with the din and the fag-smoke,
cries for a fight and calls for the sergeant,
the anger of louts for a gombeenman's farthing,—

follow the dayfall, out to the foundered
islands desired from bleak Brandon Mountain.
This is the evening. Brendan, O sailor,
stand off the mainland, backwater the glimmer;
though kirtles be flittered and flesh be seasalted,
watch! while this Ireland, a mirage, grows dimmer.
What have you come for? Why cease from faring
through paradise islands and indigo water,
through vineland and bloomland and caribbean glory?
Follow your chart with the smoking sea-monsters;
stay with the bright birds where music is pouring
balm for the hurt souls, and Judas repentant
sits for one day on a rock in the ocean.
Turn from the ghostland, O great navigator;
lower the oars for a legend
of journeys; scan tossed
empty horizons from pole to equator
for Ireland, time foundered, that Ireland has lost.

W. R. RODGERS

1909–

246   *Christ Walking on the Water*

SLOWLY, O so slowly, longing rose up
In the forenoon of his face, till only
A ringlet of fog lingered round his loins.
And fast he went down beaches all weeping
With weed, and waded out. Twelve tall waves,
Sequent and equated, hollowed and followed.
O what a cock-eyed sea he walked on,
What poke-ends of foam, what elbowings
And lugubrious looks, what ebullient

PRINTED IN GREAT BRITAIN
AT THE UNIVERSITY PRESS, OXFORD
BY VIVIAN RIDLER
PRINTER TO THE UNIVERSITY

Next morning, hearing the priest call her name,
I fled outside, being full of certainty,
And cried my seven years against the church's stone wall.
For eighteen years I did not speak her name

Until this autumn day when, in a gale,
A sapling fell outside my window, its branches
Rebelliously blotting the lawn's green. Suddenly, I thought
Of Elizabeth, frigidly stretched.

266   *Hector*

TALKING to her, he knew it was the end,
The last time he'd speed her into sleep with kisses:
Achilles had it in for him and was fighting mad.
The roads of his longing she again wandered.
A girl desirable as midsummer's day.

He was a marked man and he knew it,
Being no match for Achilles whom the gods were
    backing.
Sadly he spoke to her for hours, his heart
Snapping like sticks, she on his shoulder crying.
Yet, sorry only that the meaning eluded him,

He slept well all night, having caressed
Andromache like a flower, though in a dream he saw
A body lying on the sands, huddled and bleeding,
Near the feet a sword in bits and by the head,
An upturned, dented helmet.

267   *Time, the Faithless*

ALL evening, while the summer trees were crying
Their sudden realisation of the spring's sad death,
Somewhere a clock was ticking and we heard it here
In the sun-porch, where we sat so long, buying
Thoughts for a penny from each other. Near
Enough it was and loud to make us talk beneath our breath.

And a time for quiet talking it was, to be sure, although
The rain would have drowned the sound of our combined
        voices.
The spring of our youth that night suddenly dried
And summer filled the veins of our lives like slow
Water into creeks edging. Like the trees you cried.
Autumn and winter, you said, had so many disguises,

And how could we be always on the watch to plot
A true perspective for each minute's value? I couldn't reply,
So many of my days toppled into the past, unnoticed.
Silence like sorrow multiplied around you, a lot
Of whose days counted so much. My heart revolted
That Time for you should be such a treacherous ally,

And though, midnight inclining bells over the city
With a shower of sound like tambourines of Spain
Gay in the teeth of the night air, I thought
Of a man who said the truth was in the pity,
Somehow, under the night's punched curtain, I was lost.
I only knew the pity and the pain.

268 *Icarus*

As, even today, the airman, feeling the plane sweat
Suddenly, seeing the horizon tilt up gravely, the wings
    shiver,
Knows that, for once, Daedalus has slipped up badly,
Drunk on the job, perhaps, more likely dreaming, high-
    flier Icarus,
Head butting down, skidding along the light-shafts
Back, over the tones of the sea-waves and the slip-stream,
    heard
The gravel-voiced, stuttering trumpets of his heart

Sennet among the crumbling court-yards of his brain the
    mistake
Of trusting somebody else on an important affair like this;
And, while the flat sea, approaching, buckled into oh!
    avenues
Of acclamation, he saw the wrong story fan out into
    history,
Truth, undefined, lost in his own neglect. On the hills,
The summer-shackled hills, the sun spanged all day;
Love and the world were young and there was no ending:

But star-chaser, big-time-going, chancer Icarus
Like a dog on the sea lay and the girls forgot him,
And Daedalus, too busy hammering another job,
Remembered him only in pubs. No bugler at all
Sobbed taps for the young fool then, reported missing,
Presumed drowned, wing-bones and feathers on the tides
Drifting in casually, one by one.

MÁIRE MacENTEE

1922–

A Mhic, ná Meabhraigh Éigse

(*From the Irish*)

MY son, forsake your art,
In that which was your fathers' own no part—
Though from the start she had borne pride of place,
Poetry now leads only to disgrace.

Serve it not then, this leavings of a trade,
Nor by you be an Irish measure made,
Polished and perfect, whole in sound and sense—
Ape the new fashion, modish, cheap and dense.

Spin spineless verses of the commonplace,
Suffice it that they hold an even pace
And show not too nice taste within their span—
Preferment waits upon you if you can.

Give no man meed of censure nor just praise,
But if needs must your voice discreetly raise,
Not where there's only hatred to be earned,
Praising the Gael and for your labour spurned.

Break with them! Reckon not their histories
Nor chronicle them in men's memories,
Make it no study to enrich their fame,
Let all be named before an Irish name.

Thus you may purge your speech of bitterness,
Thus your addresses may command success—
What good repute has granted, do you hide,
Asperse their breeding, be their blood denied.

MÁIRE MacENTEE

The good that has been, see you leave alone,
That which now goes for good dilate upon;
Polish the praises of a foreign rout,
Allies more likely as has come about.

The race of Miled and the sons of Conn,
Who now maintains it, that their sway goes on?
A lying prophet in men's eyes to stand,
Proclaiming alien dynasts in the land!

The tribe of Lorc, proud Carthach's company,
Be these your strangers come from oversea,
Over Flann's ground girt with the smooth sea-ring,
Let none who bore their name bear it as king.

Conn of the Hundred Battles be forgot,
The son of Eochaidh hold you now as naught:
The stock of Conn, modest and generous,
Who had deserved a better fate from us.

Drive out of mind thought of their excellence,
Gerald's king-blood, our store of recompense,
Whom might no man for love of pelf condemn—
No poem ponder thou in praise of them.

For, since none now care,
For knowledge and the comely things that were,
And were not then like fencing in a plot,
The making of a poem shall profit not.

ROY McFADDEN

1922–

270   *Saint Francis and the Birds*

HEARING him, the birds came in a crowd,
Wing upon wing, from stone and blade and twig,
From tilted leaf and thorn and lumbering cloud,
Falling from hill, soaring from meadowland,
Wing upon widening wing, until the air
Wrinkled with sound and ran like watery sand
Round the sky's gleaming bowl. Then, like a flower
They swung, hill-blue and tremulous, each wing
A petal palpitating in a shower
Of words, till he beneath felt the stale crust
Of self crinkle and crumble and his words
Assume an independence, pure and cold,
Cageless, immaculate, one with the birds
Fattening their throats in song. Identity
Lost, he stood in swollen ecstasy.

271   *Independence*

THE sun itself was cheering, so they said;
On tiptoe in the sky, shouting hurray:
And all along the hot processional way
Laughter and songs exploded in the street
Where bombs and guns coughed blood the other day.
Dead patriots shuddered under the dancers' feet.

At last he came, his face like a black sun,
Traitor, terrorist, conspirator
Against an empire, now Prime Minister.
Silence hissed like rain as he stepped out

To say it to the straining faces there,
All ready to acclaim it with a shout.

But up there on the platform he looked small
And worn with study, exile, intrigue, jail,
Bewildered by the view inside the pale,
The years of hurt and work behind, the strong
Laws of authority now his to flail
To right or left, defining right and wrong.

And then he couldn't say it. There weren't any
Uncommitted words that could convey
Naked truths for Independence Day.
How could he *say* it when he *was* the thing?
He laughed out loud, and danced down like a gay
Enraptured child still fond enough to sing.

THOMAS KINSELLA

1927–

272   From *The Triads of Ireland*
              (*From the Irish*)

THREE accomplishments well regarded in Ireland: a clever
    verse, music on the harp, the art of shaving faces.

THREE things that foster high spirits: self-esteem, drunken-
    ness, courting.

THREE things that are always ready in a decent man's house:
    beer, a bath, a good fire.

THREE things that are always ready in a bad house: strife to confuse you, grousing, an ill-tempered hound.

THREE darknesses into which it is not right for women to go: the darkness of mist, the darkness of the night, the darkness of a wood.

The THREE deafnesses of this world: a doomed man faced with a warning, a beggar being pitied, a headstrong woman hindered in lust.

The THREE rudenesses of this world: youth mocking at age, health mocking at sickness, a wise man mocking a fool.

THREE sounds of increase: the lowing of a cow in milk, the din of a smithy, the hiss of the plough.

THREE who throw their freedom away: a lord who sells his land, a queen who takes up with a boor, a poet's son who deserts the craft.

THREE slendernesses that best hold up the world: the jet of milk into the pail, the green blade of corn in the soil, the thread spinning out of a decent woman's fist.

THREE scarcities that are better than abundance: a scarcity of fancy talk, a scarcity of cows in a small pasture, a scarcity of friends around the beer.

273   *In the Ringwood*

As I roved out impatiently
Good Friday with my bride
To drink in the rivered Ringwood
The draughty season's pride
A fell dismay held suddenly
Our feet on the green hill-side.

330

The yellow Spring on Vinegar Hill,
The smile of Slaney water,
The wind in the withered Ringwood,
Grew dark with ancient slaughter.
My love cried out and I beheld her
Change to Sorrow's daughter.

'Ravenhair, what rending
Set those red lips a-shriek,
And dealt those locks in black lament
Like blows on your white cheek,
That in your looks outlandishly
Both woe and fury speak?'

As sharp a lance as the fatal heron
There on the sunken tree
Will strike in the stones of the river
Was the gaze she bent on me.
O her robe into her right hand
She gathered grievously.

'Many times the civil lover
Climbed that pleasant place,
Many times despairing
Died in his love's face,
His spittle turned to vinegar,
Blood in his embrace.

Love that is every miracle
Is torn apart and rent.
The human turns awry
The poles of the firmament.
The fish's bright side is pierced
And good again is spent.

Though every stem on Vinegar Hill
And stone on the Slaney's bed
And every leaf in the living Ringwood
Builds till it is dead
Yet heart and hand, accomplished,
Destroy until they dread.

Dread, a grey devourer,
Stalks in the shade of love.
The dark that dogs our feet
Eats what is sickened of.
The End that stalks Beginning
Hurries home its drove.'

I kissed three times her shivering lips.
I drank their naked chill.
I watched the river shining
Where the heron wiped his bill.
I took my love in my icy arms
In the Spring on Ringwood Hill.

274   *King John's Castle*

NOT an epic, being not loosely architectured,
    But with epic force, setting the head spinning
With the taut flight earthward of its bulk, King John's
    Castle rams fast down the county of Meath.
This in its heavy ruin. New, a brute bright plateau,
    A crowded keep plunging like a bolt at Boyne water,
It held quivering under its heart a whole province of Meath.

Now the spiral stairs, man-rot of passages,
    Broken window-casements coloured with rubbed sand-
    stone,
Vertical drops chuting through three stories of masonry,
    Are a labyrinth in the medieval dark. There, peering
    behind them,
Intriguers foundered into the arms of their own monster.
    There still a spirit visits, with nothing in its embrace,
The floors of its own mildness fallen through to dust.

Life lingers latest in those blustery stone tunnels,
    A vestigial chill of desertion behind the blank face
The great rooms, the mind of the huge head, are dead.
    Views, lying inward, open on progressing phases of void,
Submarine silence, a chapel-shelf moss-grown, unreachable.
    King John directs at the river a grey stare, who once
Viewed the land in a spirit of moderation and massacre.

Contemplatives, tiny as mice moving over the green
    Mounds below, might take pleasure in the well
Of quiet there, the dark foundations near at hand.
    Up here where the wind sweeps bleakly, as though in
    remembrance
Against our own tombstones, the brave and great might
    gather.
    The blinded in spirit, whose eyes and tongues are one,
    the loving,
The cold, the crowded, the crying, this is not their fortress.

275 *Pause en route*

DEATH, when I am ready, I
Shall come; into a drowned town
Drifting, or by burning, or by
Sickness, or by striking down.

Nothing you can do can put
My coming aside, nor what I choose
To come like—holy, broken or but
An anonymity—refuse.

But, when I am ready, be
What figure you will, bloodily dressed
Or with arms held gauzily
In at my door from the tempest.

And, if your task allow it, let
The ceaseless waters take us as
One soul conversing and, if it
Deny, let that civility pass.

For little, now as then, we know
How I shall address you or
You me. Embarrassment could go
Queerly with us, scavenger.

Nothing sure—but that the brave
And proud you stopped I will not sing,
Knowing nothing of you save
A final servant functioning.

INDEX OF AUTHORS

[The references are to the numbers of the poems]

INDEX OF FIRST LINES

[The references are to the numbers of the poems]

INDEX OF FIRST LINES

INDEX OF FIRST LINES

INDEX OF FIRST LINES

INDEX OF FIRST LINES

INDEX OF FIRST LINES

INDEX OF FIRST LINES

And contumacious musics. Always there were
Hills and holes, pills and poles, a wavy wall
And bucking ribbon caterpillaring past
With glossy ease. And often, as he walked,
The slow curtains of swell swung open and showed,
Miles and smiles away, the bottle-boat
Flung on a wavering frond of froth that fell
Knee-deep and heaved thigh-high. In his forward face
No cave of afterthought opened; to his ear
No bottom clamour climbed up; nothing blinked.
For he was the horizon, he the hub,
Both bone and flesh, finger and ring of all
This clangorous sea. Docile, at his toe's touch
Each tottering dot stood roundaboutly calm
And jammed the following others fast as stone.
The ironical wave smoothed itself out
To meet him, and the mocking hollow
Hooped its back for his feet. A spine of light
Sniggered on the knobbly water, ahead.
But he like a lover, caught up,
Pushed past all wrigglings and remonstrances
And entered the rolling belly of the boat
That shuddered and lay still. And he lay there
Emptied of his errand, oozing still. Slowly
The misted mirror of his eyes grew clear
And cold, the bell of blood tolled lower,
And bright before his sight the ocean bared
And rolled its horrible bold eye-balls endlessly
In round rebuke. Looking over the edge
He shivered. Was this the way he had come?
Was that the one who came? The whole wieldy world
And all the welded welt that he had walked on
Burst like a plate into purposelessness.

All, all was gone, the fervour and the froth
Of confidence, and flat as water was
The sad and glassy round. Somewhere, then,
A tiny flute wriggled like a worm, O so lonely.
A ring of birds rose up and wound away
Into nothingness. Beyond himself he saw
The settled steeples, and breathing beaches
Running with people. But he,
He was custodian to nothing now,
And boneless as an empty sleeve hung down.
Down from crowned noon to cambered evening
He fell, fell, from white to amber, till night
Slid over him like an eyelid. And he,
His knees drawn up, his head dropped deep,
Curled like a question mark asleep.

247   *Stormy Night*

Is this the street? Never a sign of life,
The swinging lamp throws everything about;
But see! from that sly doorway, like a knife
The gilt edge of inviting light slides out
And in again—the very sign
Of her whose slightest nod I lately thought was mine;

But not now.
Knock! and the night-flowering lady
Opens, and across the brilliant sill
Sees me standing there so dark and shady
Hugging the silences of my ill-will;
Wildly she turns from me—But no, my love,
This foot's within the door, this hand's without the glove.

Well may you tremble now, and say there was nothing
    meant,
And curl away from my care with a 'Please, my dear!',
For though you were smoke, sucked up by a raging vent,
I'd follow you through every flue of your fear,
And over your faraway arms I'll mountain and cone
In a pillar of carolling fire and fountaining stone.

O strike the gong of your wrong, raise the roof of your
    rage,
Fist and foist me off with a cloud of cries,
What do I care for all your footling rampage?
On your light-in-gale blows my larking caresses will rise,
But—Why so still? What! are you weeping, my sweet?
Ah heart, heart, look! I throw myself at your feet.

248   *Life's Circumnavigators*

HERE, where the taut wave hangs
Its tented tons, we steer
Through rocking arch of eye
And creaking reach of ear,
Anchored to flying sky,
And chained to changing fear.

O when shall we, all spent,
Row in to some far strand,
And find, to our content,
The original land
From which our boat once went,
Though not the one we planned.

Us on that happy day
This fierce sea will release,
On our rough face of clay,
The final glaze of peace.
Our oars we all will lay
Down, and desire will cease.

249 *Lent*

MARY MAGDALENE, that easy woman,
Saw, from the shore, the seas
Beat against the hard stone of Lent,
Crying, 'Weep, seas, weep
For yourselves that cannot dent me more.

O more than all these, more crabbed than all stones,
And cold, make me, who once
Could leap like water, Lord. Take me
As one who owes
Nothing to what she was. Ah, naked.

My waves of scent, my petticoats of foam
Put from me and rebut;
Disown. And that salt lust stave off
That slavered me—O
Let it whiten in grief against the stones

And outer reefs of me. Utterly doff,
Nor leave the lightest veil
Of feeling to heave or soften.
Nothing cares this heart
What hardness crates it now or coffins.

Over the balconies of these curved breasts
I'll no more peep to see
The light procession of my loves
Surf-riding in to me
Who now have eyes and alcove, Lord, for Thee.'

'Room, Mary', said He, 'ah make room for me
Who am come so cold now
To my tomb.' So, on Good Friday,
Under a frosty moon
They carried Him and laid Him in her womb.

A grave and icy mask her heart wore twice,
But on the third day it thawed,
And only a stone's-flow away
Mary saw her God.
Did you hear me? Mary saw her God!

Dance, Mary Magdalene, dance, dance and sing,
For unto you is born
This day a King. 'Lady,' said He,
'To you who relent
I bring back the petticoat and the bottle of scent.'

250   *The Net*

QUICK, woman, in your net
Catch the silver I fling!
O I am deep in your debt,
Draw tight, skin-tight, the string,
And rake the silver in.
No fisher ever yet
Drew such a cunning ring.

Ah, shifty as the fin
Of any fish this flesh
That, shaken to the shin,
Now shoals into your mesh,
Bursting to be held in;
Purse-proud and pebble-hard,
Its pence like shingle showered.

Open the haul, and shake
The fill of shillings free,
Let all the satchels break
And leap about the knee
In shoals of ecstasy.
Guineas and gills will flake
At each gull-plunge of me.

Though all the Angels, and
Saint Michael at their head,
Nightly contrive to stand
On guard about your bed,
Yet none dare take a hand,
But each can only spread
His eagle-eye instead.

But I, being man, can kiss
And bed-spread-eagle too;
All flesh shall come to this,
Being less than angel is,
Yet higher far in bliss
As it entwines with you.

Come, make no sound, my sweet;
Turn down the candid lamp
And draw the equal quilt
Over our naked guilt.

ROBERT FARREN

1909–

All that is, and can Delight

In the numb time when foam froze
and sea-birds fed from the hand,
and fields like great grey paving-stones
hid green grass through the land;
when air rang to a cock's crow
as a glass to a finger nail,
we had so long sung praise of snow
we had forgotten rain:

forgotten hued and moving things:
the huge winds that bay;
waters shaken with wild fins,
and root-and-worm-rent clay.
O frost held field and cloud and surf
with still Medusal eye,
and men's eyes saw the still, stone world,
coped with the stone of the sky.

But rain teemed then from melting skies,
and wind loosed lungs of brass;
and each man, with the first man's eyes,
saw the green of grass.
And each man sang the water's praise
and the wind's praise, and lo!
we, who forgot the rain's face,
forgot the grace of snow.

Father, remind thy sons of snow
when the hedge burns with the haw;

give, while the after-grasses grow,
the whiff of a wind like a claw;
let ice, the jewel of June's light,
storm the vein with the sun;
with ray-limbed, moon-marbling night
thrill the breath from the lung.
Make all that is, and can delight,
from every atom run.

252 *The Beset Wife*

EXCELLENT work, my Hugh,
my forest bloom;
you hazard your life,
Tom haunts your wife!

What a time you're gone out
when, with watering mouth,
the robber, Jordan,
walks your garden.

The war keeps you! leave it!
Or will this evil
mountebank of Brea
cosset your wife away.

The coaxing of words together
is his profession;
long-woo'd I might weary,
and hear him.

The softest tongue in Ireland
disarms and drives me
(Hugh! home quick to me!)
drawling wittily.

Though I avoid him wildly,
he always finds me
with a new art
to hook my heart.

He comes with a hawkswoop
on my womantroop:
they beat him away
but he's there next day.

This slut in manly tunic,
with bardic music,
with charm of druidry,
lacks naught to ruin me.

I declare to you, O Rourke
he feigns your very look,
your low, dear voice
And even your eyes.

And then with his own bright face
sets my blood a-race.
'Twill carry my love
astray on its flood,

unless you ferret and find,
within your mind,
some master-trick.
I am wax to his wick!

I can't be wife to you both.
My bridal troth
is yours yet, Hugh.
Ah Tom! but you?

Unless you want me weeping,
Jordan, leave me.
Yielding to you
I'd murder Hugh.

You boast of blood that flows
From Costello's:
pair this pomp of blood
with maidenhood.

Shall Breiffne's wife be still a
frail Dervorgilla
and *my* O Rourke
rue pledges broke?

Midsummer mist are you
my Sun bursts through.
O be it sung:
when I was young

he harvested my love like wheat.
Be it still sweet
and clean, without weed
of black deed.

Behind your counterfeit face
the smart scapegrace
with brazen grin,
praising sin.

Think! if you feed the fire
of loose desire,
Hell-fire's
fed as well.

O head of Absalom sunned
in a scented wood,
my golden Hugh
Out Absaloms you.

O summed splendour of men!
court you again
with Guaire's Wealth
Finbar's slimy stealth,

MacAirt's philosophy,
Finn's sagacity,
Aengus of Brugh's
eyes like dew?

O hammering hand in warfare!
heel of a hare
on the running-ground!
O billow-bound,

slaughterous, on enemies!
silk cord of peace!
abounding pool!
great orchard full!

Hugh you are half betrayed,
your foe's praised. . . .
Here, God of Grace,
He's here!

Race, Tom, no more good-byeing
(daft heart hush crying!)
and no more turning. . . .

Hugh
a mhuirnín![1]

[1] Sweetheart.

253   *No Woman Born*

YOUNG head in sunlight! Not a woman born
has lifted head like her head; plenty's horn
poured no alight abundance like her hair.
Wonder is on her lids like the bright air.
She wakes to worship, and draws on dull mouths to prayer.
There is, to be named one with her, no woman born.

254   *The Mason*

NOTHING older than stone but the soil and the sea and the
    sky.
Nothing stronger than stone but water and air and fire.
Nothing worthier than stone but the harpstring, the word
    and the tree.
Nothing humbler or stubborner than stone—whatever
    it be!

Stone is the bone of the world, under moor, under loam,
under ocean and churchyard-corruption of buried bone;
floor of the mountain, pound of the ocean, the world's
    cord.
God's creature, stone, that once was the vault of its Lord.

God gave me stone to know for a womb with child,
the time of delivery come but waiting the knife:
I free the stone-born glory into the air,
rounded and grooved and edged and grained and rare.

I have mastered the grain, the make, the temper of stone,
fingering it and considering, touching with hand and with
    soul,
quarrying it out of the course, piercing and severing it,
with a chirp of meeting metals like a bird's chirp.

Basalt I know—bottle-green still pools of stone
harder than hawk's beak, shark's tooth or tusk of the boar;
basalt—the glass-stone, stone without pore or wart;
causeway-stone stepped across Moyle-fjord in the north.

Granite I know—dust-pearl with silver eyes—
that moulds domed hills, with snow, rain, wind and time.
Marble—the multiple-tinted—the satin-flesh—
daughter of the King of white Greece in the lands of the
    west.

Dark flint I know with the feel of a fox's tongue,
the unconsumed cold carrier of fire its young,
stone of hairedges and thornpoints, the dagger stone,
spearstone, swordstone, hatchet-stone, hearth-gilly stone.

O Christ, the stone which the builders rejected
and which is become the head of the corner,
part me from them the stone shall grind when it fall;
leave me not a stone in thine enemies' hand!

255   *The Pets*

> COLM had a cat,
> and a wren,
> and a fly.
>
> The cat was a pet,
> and the wren,
> and the fly.

And it happened that the wren
ate the fly;
and it happened that the cat
ate the wren.

Then the cat died.

So Saint Colm lacked a cat
and a wren,
and a fly.

But Saint Colm loved the cat,
and the wren,
and the fly,

so he prayed to get them back,
cat and wren;
and he prayed to get them back,
wren and fly.

And the cat became alive
and delivered up the wren;
and the wren became alive
and delivered up the fly;
and they all lived with Colm
till the day came to die.

First the cat died.
Then the wren died.
Then the fly.

BRIAN O NOLAN

1911–

(Translations from the Irish)

Aoibhinn, a leabhráin, do thriall

DELIGHTFUL, book, your trip
to her of the ringlet head,
a pity it's not you
that's pining, I that sped.

To go, book, where she is
delightful trip in sooth!
the bright mouth red as blood
you'll see, and the white tooth.

You'll see that eye that's grey
the docile palm as well,
with all that beauty you
(not I, alas) will dwell.

You'll see the eyebrow fine
the perfect throat's smooth gleam,
and the sparkling cheek I saw
latterly in a dream.

The lithe good snow-white waist
That won mad love from me—
the handwhite swift neat foot—
These in their grace you'll see.

The soft enchanting voice
that made me each day pine
you'll hear, and well for you—
would that your lot were mine.

315

257   *Scel lem duib*

HERE'S a song—
stags give tongue
winter snows
summer goes.

High cold blow
sun is low
brief his day
seas give spray.

Fern clumps redden
shapes are hidden
wildgeese raise
wonted cries.

Cold now girds
wings of birds
icy time—
that's my rime.

DONAGH MacDONAGH
1912–

258   *A Warning to Conquerors*

THIS is the country of the Norman tower,
The graceless keep, the bleak and slitted eye
Where fear drove comfort out; straw on the floor
Was price of conquering security.

They came and won, and then for centuries
Stood to their arms; the face grew bleak and lengthened
In the night vigil, while their foes at ease
Sang of the strangers and the towers they strengthened.

Ragweed and thistle hold the Norman field
And cows the hall where Gaelic never rang
Melodiously to harp or spinning-wheel.
Their songs are spent now with the voice that sang;

And lost their conquest. This soft land quietly
Engulfed them like the Saxon and the Dane—
But kept the jutted brow, the slitted eye;
Only the faces and the names remain.

259   *The Hungry Grass*

CROSSING the shallow holdings high above sea
Where few birds nest, the luckless foot may pass
From the bright safety of experience
Into the terror of the hungry grass.

Here in a year when poison from the air
First withered in despair the growth of spring
Some skull-faced wretch whom nettle could not save
Crept on four bones to his last scattering,

Crept, and the shrivelled heart which drove his thought
Towards platters brought in hospitality
Burst as the wizened eyes measured the miles
Like dizzy walls forbidding him the city.

Little the earth reclaimed from that poor body,
And yet remembering him the place has grown
Bewitched and the thin grass he nourishes
Racks with his famine, sucks marrow from the bone.

Dublin Made Me

DUBLIN made me and no little town
With the country closing in on its streets
The cattle walking proudly on its pavements
The jobbers, the gombeenmen and the cheats

Devouring the fair-day between them
A public-house to half a hundred men
And the teacher, the solicitor and the bank-clerk
In the hotel bar drinking for ten.

Dublin made me, not the secret poteen still
The raw and hungry hills of the West
The lean road flung over profitless bog
Where only a snipe could nest

Where the sea takes its tithe of every boat.
Bawneen and currach have no allegiance of mine,
Nor the cute self-deceiving talkers of the South
Who look to the East for a sign.

The soft and dreary midlands with their tame canals
Wallow between sea and sea, remote from adventure,
And Northward a far and fortified province
Crouches under the lash of arid censure.

I disclaim all fertile meadows, all tilled land
The evil that grows from it and the good,
But the Dublin of old statutes, this arrogant city,
Stirs proudly and secretly in my blood.

261   *Going to Mass Last Sunday*

(Tune: *The Lowlands of Holland*)

GOING to Mass last Sunday my true love passed me by,
I knew her mind was altered by the rolling of her eye;
And when I stood in God's dark light my tongue could
    word no prayer
Knowing my saint had fled and left her reliquary bare.

Sweet faces smiled from holy glass, demure in saintly love,
Sweet voices ripe with Latin grace rolled from the choir
    above;
But brown eyes under Sunday wear were all my liturgy;
How can she hope for heaven who has so deluded me?

When daffodils were altar gold her lips were light on mine
And when the hawthorn flame was bright we drank the
    year's new wine;
The nights seemed stained-glass windows lit with love that
    paled the sky,
But love's last ember perishes in the winter of her eye.

Drape every downcast day now in purple cloth of Lent,
Smudge every forehead now with ash, that she may yet
    repent,
Who going to Mass last Sunday could pass so proudly by
And show her mind was altered by the rolling of an eye.

262 *On the Bridge of Athlone: A Prophecy*

I SEE them a mother and daughter
At dusk in a grass-grown lane
An old road from nowhere to nowhere
Where time has been slain
A mother and daughter ragged
And brown as a bird on a tree
Hair tangled and coarse as the bushes
Eye clear as the sea
And the land is a sea all about them
A green sea of grasses and trees
A pole like the mast of a wrecked ship
Trails its wires in the breeze
And the only things living are insects
And rabbits grown strong again
And the women haggard as madmen
From hunger and rain
And the daughter comes running and crying
—I saw on the Bridge of Athlone
A man O mother a man there
And he's passed and is gone—
And men are so few now in Ireland
That mother and daughter cry
As one might mourn the last angel
A kingfisher gone by
And they weep for the land that is desolate
Green and empty that once was hard won
Lot's daughters with no Lot and no wine-cup
To get them a son.

LESLIE DAIKEN

1912–

263 *Lines to my Father*

YOU have not left me usurer's black blood
Nor legacy of bawdry or disgrace,
Yet against your own improvidence you could
Have schooled me. You, whose peasant's face,
Grained with the sweat of some grim charioteer,
Disdained to tame fresh horses into fear,
But scared the gazers with high-stepping grace.
Old jobstock-man, you drove with foxy zeal
A merchant's hard, but never haggling deal:
Here, split a sovereign; there, not a fraction budge
From your inflexible rockbottom fudge
Till those brisk hands, chapped and weather-bit,
Clapped, palm on palm, their stamp of friendly spit
In every City metal-yard or any country pub
And the glass of malt had method. . . . Aye, there's the rub
Dead Father! . . . Peace on you, hoarding spendthrift!
Your gambler's blood is in me. Let me drift
Then, down my poet's millrace—to what end?—
Who failed to break a son into a friend.

NIALL SHERIDAN

1912–

264 *Ad Lesbiam*

(*From the Latin of Catullus*)

HOW many kisses, Lesbia, you ask,
Would serve to sate this hungry love of mine?
—As many as the Libyan sands that bask
Along Cyrene's shore where pine trees wave,

Where burning Jupiter's untended shrine
Lies near to old King Battus' sacred grave:
Let them be endless as the stars at night
That stare upon the lovers in a ditch—
So often would love-crazed Catullus bite
Your burning lips, that prying eye should not
Have power to count, nor evil tongues bewitch
The frenzied kisses that you gave and got.

VALENTIN IREMONGER
1918–

265   *This Houre Her Vigill . . .*

ELIZABETH, frigidly stretched,
On a spring day surprised us
With her starched dignity and the quietness
Of her hands clasping a black cross.

With book and candle and holy-water dish
She received us in the room with the blind down.
Her eyes were peculiarly closed and we knelt shyly,
Noticing the blot of her hair on the white pillow.

We met that evening by the crumbling wall
In the field behind the house where I lived
And talked it over but could find no reason
Why she had left us whom she had liked so much.

Death, yes, we understood: something to do
With age and decay, decrepit bodies.
But here was this vigorous one aloof and prim
Who would not answer our furtive whispers.